WELLINGTON

WELLINGTON

Reproduced by special permission of His Grace The Duke of Wellington, K.G.
From the painting by Sir Thomas Lawrence at Apsley House.

WELLINGTON

BY

THE HON. JOHN FORTESCUE, LL.D., D.LITT.

AUTHOR OF "A HISTORY OF THE BRITISH ARMY," ETC.

PORTRAIT AND MAPS

NEW YORK

DODD, MEAD & COMPANY

1925

To

ARTHUR

FOURTH DUKE OF WELLINGTON

THIS SKETCH OF HIS ILLUSTRIOUS GRANDFATHER

IS GRATEFULLY DEDICATED

CONTENTS

CHAPTER I

CHAPTER II

CONTENTS

CHAPTER III

[viii]

CONTENTS

[ix]

CONTENTS

CHAPTER IV

CONTENTS

CHAPTER V

[xi]

CONTENTS

CONTENTS

[xiii]

CONTENTS

[xiv]

CONTENTS

ILLUSTRATIONS

CHAPTER I

THE family of Wellesley appears to trace its origin to Devon, the name having passed from its primitive form of Westleigh through the corruptions of Westley and Wesley before it assumed, little more than a century ago, its present familiar shape. There is evidence that a Wellesley was already in Ireland in the thirteenth century. The family of Colley is conjectured to have come from Gloucestershire; and a branch of it was settled in Ireland early in the sixteenth century. No man bearing either name seems to have attained to any great prominence in the Irish branch until, in 1746, Richard Colley of Castle Carbury, Kildare, was created a peer of Ireland. Having in 1728 succeeded to the estates of his cousin, Garrett Wesley of Dangan and Mornington, in County Meath, he took the additional surname of Wesley, and chose for his title the Barony of Mornington. Upon his death he was succeeded by his son Garrett, who in 1760 was advanced in the peerage by the titles of Earl of Mornington and Viscount Wellesley. He is said to have owed his promotion to his musical

[1]

talents, which commended him to the favour of George III, himself an enthusiast over music. Undoubtedly he possessed unusual gifts in the most emotional of the arts, and his name survives as the composer of double-chants and of one or two glees to this day.

This musical Lord Mornington married Anne Hill, daughter of Arthur, first Viscount Dungannon, who bore him nine children: Richard, afterwards Marquess Wellesley, born in 1760; William, later Lord Maryborough, born in 1763; two sons, Arthur and Francis, who died in early boyhood; a daughter, Anne, born in 1768; Arthur, the future Duke of Wellington, born on some uncertain day at the very end of April or beginning of May 1769; Gerald, later a prebendary of Durham, born in 1770; a second daughter, Mary, born in 1772, who died in 1794; and Henry, later Lord Cowley, born in 1773.

Lady Mornington is said to have been a cold and austere woman; but, if a portrait of her in old age can be trusted as a guide, she must have been remarkably beautiful, which would be enough to attract any Wellesley, let alone one with a touch of musical genius. In any case, if she spoiled any of her children, it must have been the eldest, a brilliant and beautiful boy: certainly it was not Arthur. We know little of Arthur's childhood, but enough to be sure that it was not happy. He was not very strong physically, and was shy and unsociable. Possibly he was rather over-powered by his elder brothers, and he seems to have received no more sympathy from his sister than from his mother. He inherited his father's love of music, and learned to play the violin with some skill; but his father died when the boy was twelve years old, and any kindly influence that may have flowed from him was lost. The lad was driven back upon himself; and the key of his character became self-repression.

In the matter of education Arthur was sent first to a preparatory school at Chelsea and then to Eton; but his mother's means were too scanty to permit him to stay at Eton after his father's death, and she took him away with her to Brussels, where he received private tuition. Lady Mornington then decided that her "ugly boy" was fit food for powder, and in 1786 she sent him to a military academy, which was principally a riding-school, at Angers. Here he remained for about a year, when, through the interest of his brother, Lord Mornington, he obtained a commission as ensign in the

Seventy-third Highlanders, then serving in India.
So far he had learned at least to speak and write
French, if not with perfect idiomatic correctness,
at least with facility and resolution, and to acquire
a rather ugly seat on a horse.

Within six months of donning the red coat, in
November 1787, he was appointed aide-de-camp
to two Lords-Lieutenant of Ireland, first the Duke
of Buckingham and later Lord Westmorland,
remaining on that staff until March 1793. Meanwhile, as was the fashion in those days, he passed
rapidly from regiment to regiment in the way of
promotion. On the 25th of December 1787 he
was advanced to a lieutenancy into the Seventy-
sixth Foot, which was just coming to birth as one
of four new regiments raised for service in India.
By this manœuvre, no doubt, he obtained his
lieutenancy without purchase, but, as he had no
wish to proceed to India, he exchanged on the 23rd
of January 1788 into the Forty-first, then in process
of transformation from a corps of Invalids into a
regular regiment of the Line, and therefore also
containing a few subalterns who had not bought
their commissions. Finally, on the 25th of June
in the same year, he was transferred to the Twelfth
Light Dragoons, whereby he secured the con-

[4]

venience of belonging to a regiment which was, and indeed for nearly seventy years had been, quartered in Ireland. On their muster-rolls he remained for three years, until on the 30th of June 1791 he obtained a company in the Fifty-eighth Foot, once again apparently without purchase and possibly by the favour of the Lord-Lieutenant, for the Fifty-eighth was on the Irish establishment. On the 31st of October 1792 he was transferred to the Eighteenth Light Dragoons, also quartered in Ireland at that time, and so accomplished his sixth change of regiments within five years.

Whether he did regimental duty with any of these corps is extremely doubtful. Some of them perhaps he never joined nor even saw, but he probably presented himself at the depot of the Seventy-third, and he certainly was for a time with the Fifty-eighth. It may have been there that he caused a private to be weighed, with and without his kit and accoutrements, so as to judge of the burden that the soldier was expected to carry. There, too, he may have mastered his drill before he betook himself to Dublin Castle; but, once within those precincts, it is unlikely that he entered a barrack-yard again. Meanwhile, life on the staff of the Lord-Lieutenant can hardly

have been congenial to a shy and sheepish young
man. He varied it by entering the Irish Parliament as member for the borough of Trim in 1790,
and is said to have won popularity among his
constituents by his excellent temper, his firmness,
and his amiable manners. The experience was
doubtless of value to him; but meanwhile the life
was expensive, and his private income did not
exceed £125 a year. It is said that he ran into
debt, and that his chief, Lord Buckingham, came
to his assistance; and it is certain that to the end
of his life he showed particular affability to the
Grenvilles and to their relations. A more serious
matter was that he fell in love with Lady Katherine
Pakenham, and became engaged to her, though
lack of means upon both sides forbade them marry.
Altogether the first five years of his life as a soldier
were passed in a fashion which would by no means
commend itself to a modern commanding officer.

And yet it must be said for him that there was
little that was attractive in the military profession at
that period. For the British soldier, the ten years
that intervened between the end of the American
rebellion and the beginning of the war of the
French Revolution were among the very worst in
history. In the first place, the army had returned

from America defeated and discredited. The war had been enormously costly, and the first and most natural economy was to reduce the military forces to the lowest possible strength. This would have signified less if any pains had been taken to maintain their efficiency, whatever their numerical weakness; but, on the contrary, they were allowed to fall absolutely to pieces. The pay of the private soldier was literally insufficient to keep him from starvation, and the result was that recruits could hardly be obtained, or, if beguiled into accepting the shilling, deserted immediately. In Ireland, particularly, the average number of deserters amounted to one-sixth of the whole establishment. Thus, weak though the regiments would have been even if their ranks had been filled, they were weaker still from want of recruits. In other words, the officers had no men to command. It must be remembered, too, that regiments were rarely kept together in those days. In England there were, except in a few fortresses—such as the Tower,—no barracks, and the men were billeted in small bodies, often no more than troops or companies, in the ale-houses of provincial towns. In Ireland there were barracks, but these were mostly small and widely distributed, so as to enable the troops to do the work of police. In either country it might take a colonel a day's journey to visit the whole of his regiment. Thus there was every facility for slackness on the part of the officers, and every difficulty in the way of a commander who disapproved of such slackness.

Moreover, there were plenty of colonels who gave themselves no trouble about their regiments; and, despite of periodic inspections by generals, it was almost impossible to stir such commanding officers into activity. A colonel was the proprietor of his regiment, having paid hard cash for it, and, within certain limits, did very much what was right in his own eyes. Even in the matter of drill no uniformity was enforced until March 1792. A colonel might be an able and enthusiastic soldier who gave his men training that was far in advance of his time, or he might be a hard-thinking old dullard who was quite content if his battalion could blunder through the prescribed movements somehow. At the best, all that was expected of a battalion or a regiment of cavalry was extreme precision of drill with, in the case of the infantry, very exact performance of the manual and firing exercise. With the old musket the average number of misfires was forty per cent.; and only extraordinary care in loading could keep that average below fifty or sixty per cent. For this reason good commanders worked to make the business of loading a matter of mechanical habit, so that their men should go through it as coolly in the heat of action as on parade; but even so the first volley, which had been loaded carefully before the engagement, was jealously husbanded, for it was bound to be more effective than any that should subsequently be fired.

But here it must be noted that in respect of musketry the British were far ahead of any army in Europe. During the War of American Independence they had been called upon to meet an elusive enemy, who had carried marksmanship in civil life to a high degree of perfection; and they had been obliged to adapt themselves to that enemy's tactics. The result had been not only great improvement in shooting, but a definite and far-reaching change in tactical formation. Hitherto the British infantry, even as all the infantry of Europe, had been drawn up three ranks deep for action, the front rank kneeling and the two rear ranks firing over their heads. In America the British soon learned to fight in two ranks only, frequently also loosening their formation to encounter scattered sharp-shooters in woodland fighting. This formation in double rank, though not laid down by regulation, became the rule after the end of the war, and it signified the very important fact that, given an equal number of men, the British front of fire was longer than that of any other nation. The soundness of the lessons learned in America had been tested against French regular troops in St Lucia in 1778. There thirteen hundred British soldiers, fresh from active service in America, repulsed twelve thousand French, inflicting upon them a loss of four hundred killed and twelve hundred wounded. This in itself was a notable performance, but the engagement presented one very remarkable feature. At the height of the action the British ammunition failed, and it was thought best to reserve the one or two rounds left to each man for a final effort. The order was therefore given to cease fire, and it was instantly obeyed. Men who had their muskets to their shoulders and their fingers on the trigger in all the heat of combat, brought their weapons down without hesitation undischarged. I know of no finer example of fire-discipline in all military history; and no doubt it was quoted as such in the army.

This was the supreme achievement of military

training over the very rude material of which the British Army was composed. That better material should be obtained under existing conditions was not to be expected. In barracks the men were infamously housed, being huddled together by fours in wooden cribs to sleep, and having only their sleeping-rooms in which to do everything but their drill. They drank hard, as did every class at that time, and they could buy fiery spirits in the barrack-yard; it being judged impossible to prevent them from smuggling liquor into their quarters, and therefore a less evil to permit them to purchase it. There was no encouragement to good behaviour; and one principal punishment, merciless flogging, was inflicted for misconduct. They were, on the other hand, always officers who sought, and with great success, to rule their men with kindness and consideration; but their great difficulty was that they could not afford to rid themselves of bad characters. A soldier was enlisted for life, and, if he were discharged, he must be replaced, which was a matter of expense to the officers, for the country did not grant bounty enough to attract recruits. In 1790, for instance, an alarm of war with Spain led to sudden augmentation of the army. The Treasury offered a bounty of five guineas; but the actual price of recruits rose to fifteen guineas. Hence officers were obliged by sheer penury to keep not only undesirable men, but decrepit old veterans who could hardly stand on their legs and were utterly useless except on parade. It was not that they wilfully defrauded their country, but that the Treasury, by its extreme niggardliness, forced such fraud upon them.

And the officers had other grievances, of which the most serious was that they were wholly under civil control. There was no Commander-in-Chief, only a civilian Secretary at War, who, as was natural, conducted all his business with the main object of securing votes. There were an Adjutant-General and a Quartermaster-General, who, technically, were on the immediate staff of the King; but there was no one to press upon Ministers the grievances and the requirements of officers and men. Apart from the prohibitive expense of recruits, the pay of subalterns of cavalry was, owing to the high price of forage, scarcely equal to the maintenance of their servants and their horses; and the result was that vacant cornetcies could not be filled. The pay of an officer gave him only an absurdly trifling sum over and above the interest on the price of his commission; and it was too much to expect that gentlemen should invest money in a dead loss. The Adjutant-General in vain pressed the hard case both of these subalterns and of the private soldier upon the Chancellor of the Exchequer. But William Pitt, who was busy with the task of putting the finances of the country on a sound basis—in itself a transcendent service,—turned a deaf ear. In 1792 he did improve the position of the private soldier so far as not only to deliver him from starvation, but actually to allow him the munificent sum of a trifle under one penny one farthing a day; but this he did at the cost of leaving the subalterns unrelieved. The general result of Pitt's parcimony and of civilian control of the army was that discipline among the officers was extremely bad. Colonels could not be hard upon their officers for not keeping the ranks of their companies full, when they literally could not afford to pay the cost of recruits; and a subaltern took little account of his military superiors when, if he were refused leave of absence by them, he could obtain it, through political influence, directly from the Secretary at War.

Such, very briefly, was the state of the army, or rather of the group of self-dependent regiments which was called the army, when Arthur Wellesley joined it, and when the war of the French Revolution and Empire began. By the end of 1792 the revolutionary government of France, having landed the country in bankruptcy, set out to indemnify itself by the plunder of its neighbours; and Holland, rich in money but absolutely effete in government and military efficiency, was their first object. Though Pitt counted upon the destruction of French trade over sea as the surest means of vanquishing France, and, to that end, sent most of the meagre British battalions to the West Indies, he could not refuse a small contingent to join the Austrians in driving the French out of the Austrian Netherlands, and in thus saving not only the bank of Amsterdam but the port of Antwerp from falling into French hands. War was declared on the 7th of February 1793, and by the end of March two weak brigades, one of the Guards, the other of the Line, had been landed in Holland, to serve, together with a contingent of Hanoverians and hired Hessians, under the Duke of York, subject to the supreme direction of an Austrian Commander-in-Chief.

In that same month of March Arthur Wellesley begged his elder brother, Mornington, to advance him the money for purchase of a majority in the

Thirty-third. Mornington did so, afterwards refusing to accept repayment; and Arthur, having
become major on the 30th of April, was further
promoted lieutenant-colonel, with command of the
regiment, on the 30th of September. As to the
condition of the Thirty-third at the time we know
nothing, but, if it were not weak in numbers, it
must have been full, in common with all other
regiments, of bad recruits. Meanwhile, the campaign of 1793 in the Low Countries had been
wrecked by the failure of the Duke of York's siege
of Dunkirk, a fatuous operation which had been
forced upon him by Ministers in the hope of making the war popular. The campaign of 1794,
after a brilliant little success or two, went even
worse. The Austrians deliberately exposed the
Duke of York's troops to certain defeat at the
Battle of Tourcoing (18th of May) in order to give
themselves an excuse for evacuating the Netherlands. By the middle of June they had already
left the British contingent in isolation on the
Scheldt; and the British war minister, whose one
idea of conducting operations was to hold on
tightly to the port of Ostend, hurried thither three
regiments from Ireland, the Thirty-third among
them, together with eight more battalions and a

large body of drafts—in all, about ten thousand
men—under Lord Moira. The first batch of these
reinforcements reached Ostend on the 21st of
June; on the 25th the Thirty-third disembarked
after a passage of nineteen days from Cork; and
on the 26th arrived the remainder of the troops,
together with Moira himself.

These must have been some of the strangest
British soldiers ever seen. The drafts arrived
without arms or military appointments of any
kind; and it was only through the accident of a
fog at sea, which delayed the sailing of some of
the transports, that a complete battalion was not
landed in precisely the same condition. All of
Moira's regiments had been skimmed to fill the
empty ranks of other corps, which had been sent
to man the fleet, or to the West Indies; and six
of them, including the Thirty-third, had been
stripped of their finest men by the detachment of
their flank-companies upon another service. Pitt,
moreover, had resorted to a vile expedient of his
father's to raise men, by offering rank in the army
to any young man of means who undertook to
produce a given number of recruits, so many for
an ensigncy, so many for a lieutenancy, and so
forth. There was a perfect rush for these com-

missions. Army-brokers, who carried on a most scandalous traffic for their purchase and exchange, contrived to raise not only schoolboys but gambling-house keepers and other most undesirable characters to the rank of field-officers. Arthur Wellesley had just sufficient seniority to escape the degradation of being subjected to the command of these worthless creatures; but other deserving old officers were not so fortunate, and found themselves suddenly, and through no fault of their own, subordinate to men undistinguished by birth or intellect, and totally ignorant of their profession. And the new recruits were as bad as the new officers. They were the offscourings of the nation, who could be purchased at a cheap rate by the crimps—criminals, decrepit old men, raw boys, the half-witted, the feeble-minded, and even downright lunatics. All of them were untrained, and not a few untrainable. "Many of them do not know one end of a firelock from the other," wrote the Duke of York's chief staff-officer, "and will never know it."

With regiments composed of such men under such officers, Lord Moira was expected to hold Ostend, an indefensible place, against a greatly superior force of French, the advanced guard of which lay only four miles away. Happily the enemy made no immediate attempt to molest him, and he slipped off to Ghent, joining the Duke of York on the 6th of July a few miles further to the east. Three weeks later the Austrians finally parted from the Duke, who thereupon retired into Holland with some forty thousand men, twenty-five thousand of them British, that were left to him. The French numbered about one hundred and fifty thousand; and the task set to the Duke was to manœuvre over a wide front to hold an army four times as great as his own in check. We have seen something of the officers and men of the Duke's force, and it remains to say a few words of the higher command and of the departments. The Duke himself, though later he proved himself an excellent administrator at home, was of no use in the field, though he had a very competent adviser in Colonel James Craig. There were only four generals, including those on the staff. Transport and supply was the business of the Commissariat, a department of the Treasury, and was carried on chiefly through contractors. There was also a newly raised transport-corps called the Royal Waggon Train. But the officials of the Treasury naturally knew nothing about supplying an army in the

[18]

field; and the Waggon Train, whose nickname in the army was the "Newgate Blues," was composed chiefly of convicts. To complicate the matter of transport, the new officers, in order to make themselves comfortable, hired innumerable private waggons under the charge of insubordinate drivers, which swelled the baggage columns to unmanageable dimensions. The medical department was perhaps worst of all, the staff being made up, for economy's sake, of drunken apothecaries, broken-down practitioners, and every description of rogue; and the sick and wounded were infamously treated. The hospitals were known in the army as the "shambles"; and wounded men were sent back to England in the depth of winter on the bare upper decks of ships, with no protection against the weather, and without even straw to lie upon. Even the artillery, which is rarely found wanting, was deficient in this army. There were plenty of guns and plenty of horses, but few trained gunners, and no drivers at all. We find Arthur Wellesley himself supplying ten drivers from the Thirty-third. The state of the army in which he first saw active service was, indeed, almost incredible.

There is no need to follow its dismal story closely, the less so since we know next to nothing of Arthur

Wellesley's part in it. He came under fire for the first time at Bokstel on the 15th of September, and we have one letter from him which shows him in a state of anxious vigilance, having not taken his clothes off for days. He had good reason for his anxiety, for he hardly saw a general from end to end of the campaign. To make a long story short, the Duke of York was slowly pushed back, until at the end of November he seemed to be safe on the north side of the Waal. Then the weather turned bitterly cold, and the troops fell down fast, for, in fact, of the nineteen British battalions that had reinforced the Duke of York's army in 1794, not one had any greatcoats. The force in British pay had already shrunk to twenty-one thousand; and of these, eleven thousand were on the sick-list. Through alternations of frost and thaw they held their position, fighting not a few spirited little actions, and then drew back behind the next river to northward, until that also was frozen, and it was necessary to retreat north-eastward to the Yssel. Hardship and neglect had utterly destroyed discipline. The officers who had raised recruits for rank took no care of their men, but remained drinking after the columns had marched, and then came galloping up, full of wine and careless where they rode. Four were tried by court-martial for cowardice after a single skirmish. The country was poor and inhospitable at best, and was now covered with snow, twice thawed and refrozen. There was little fuel and little food, and the British fought pitched battles with the German mercenaries for what there was. On the morning of the second day of the retreat such men as rose from the bivouac saw nothing around them for miles but hundreds of men and horses frozen to death. On the fourth day they reached shelter and comparative plenty, but after ten days' halt they were obliged by scarcity to retire again to the Ems. When they reached it the number of fighting men had shrunk to six thousand. It was the most terrible retreat that British Army had ever made. Had it lasted four days longer hardly a man would have survived.

Through all this, with its privations, its horrors and distresses, Arthur Wellesley passed, and left not one word of his experiences behind him. One English account alone was written at the time, and the campaign for more than a century remained unknown. Officers shrank from recalling a period of such misery and disgrace; and Arthur Wellesley doubtless shared the general feeling. When once

[21]

or twice questioned on the subject, he answered
that at least he learned how things should not be
done; but he learned far more than this. The
value of the few disciplined old soldiers that
leavened the general rabble of recruits must have
been brought home to him; and not less instructive
must have been the many little encounters with the
tumultuous swarms of the French infantry. They,
too, were as yet but a half-trained mob, living on
the country, which necessarily meant marauding
and bad discipline, and trusting in combat mainly
to headlong rushes of dense columns with the bayonet. Again and again small parties of the British
had repulsed their attacks, and had more than once
counter-attacked with success. The inference was
plain that the shock-action of columns could be met
by the missile-action of lines. The men, though ill-
led, had behaved well; and it was not difficult to
imagine what might be the prowess of a long firing-
line of perfectly disciplined soldiers under competent officers It was plain that the teaching of the
American War was good and sound; and there
were veterans enough from that war to pass on the
lesson to the Duke of York's army.

A thinking officer, moreover—and Arthur Wellesley though young, was already a thinking man,

—would realise that an army with its supply-service properly organised must always have the better of one that lives on the country. In the first place, living on the country almost inevitably signifies oppression of the inhabitants, which makes them hostile, and therefore dangerous in case of a reverse. In the second place, the men are practically encouraged to robbery and pillage, which apart from the evil to discipline, gives the stronger men plenty and leaves the weaker, who are less able to fend for themselves, to go in scarceness. In the third place, an army, if it is to gather its subsistence as it advances, must be widely dispersed, and must therefore cover greater distances, often by forced marches, in order to concentrate for action. Forced marches mean great strain upon the men, or in plain words, casualties. Briefly, therefore, an army with proper organised supply-service pays for its provisions in cash; an army which lives on the plunder of the country pays for them with men's lives. The French under the Revolution followed the latter system, because they had no money, and were virtually compelled to keep their armies on foreign soil in order to preserve them alive; and Napoleon followed the revolutionary tradition to the end. England being richer always in cash than in men, in general, followed the opposite system, especially under that great and wise leader, John, Duke of Marlborough. It is possible that Wellesley did not formulate his opinions exactly as here expressed. Possibly he put them to himself more tersely still; but I cannot doubt that he sailed from the Ems for England in the spring of 1795 with two military principles firmly impressed upon his mind, namely, the vital importance of an efficient supply and transport-service, and the tactical value of missile-action against shock-action. Lastly, he took to heart until the very end of his life the unfitness of any but the better class of Englishman to hold an officer's commission. "Your army is destroyed," wrote the Hanoverian general, Walmoden, to the Duke of York at the end of the retreat. "The officers, their carriages, and a large train are safe, but the men are destroyed." It was a terrible indictment, but it was true; and Wellington never forgot the consequences of scattering commissions broadcast to any man or child who could afford to satisfy the demands of the crimps. Men who in after years talked sneeringly of the old Duke's prejudices against officers of humble birth never knew or never thought of his first campaign, nor of the retreat to the Ems.

[24]

CHAPTER II

WELLESLEY returned home in advance of the army, the main body of which remained on the Ems until the middle of April 1795. In June he applied to the Lord-Lieutenant of Ireland for employment in a civil department, not because he preferred civil to military duty, but because he had observed that "the manner in which military offices were filled" gave no chance to him. His request was not granted, and he rejoined his regiment at Warley, in Essex, embarking with it in November for the West Indies as part of an expedition under the command of Sir Ralph Abercromby. The transports sailed from Portsmouth on the 16th of November, and were driven back by a gale, not without the total loss of several ships, on the 18th. They started again on the 3rd of December, Wellesley as well as Abercromby taking a passage in the *Glory,* flagship of Admiral Christian, who held the chief naval command. After seven weeks' vain battling with foul weather, the *Glory* was blown back to Portsmouth for the second time before she had even got clear of the Channel. About thirty transports, among them those which carried the Thirty-third, also returned to different ports in England, and about a hundred more were dispersed, whither no man could tell. Most of them found their way to the West Indies, where Abercromby and such troops as were with him, eventually overtook them in March. The Thirty-third was, however, detained for four months at Poole, and eventually disembarked in England. Had the first voyage been prosperous, Wellesley would have found himself to be one of five officers who alone knew their business amid the wretched rabble which was called Abercromby's army. One of these, Abercromby himself, he was never to see again; two more, John Moore and John Hope, he was to meet later in the Peninsula. Had he been with them he would have learned much, supposing that he had survived the operations which resulted in the recapture of St Vincent, Grenada, and St Lucia. Few did survive them. John Moore himself was actually wrapped in his shroud for burial when he was snatched out of the jaws of yellow fever; and Arthur Wellesley might have been less fortunate than Moore. But he would certainly have gained distinction if he had lived, and the experience of a West Indian campaign would have completed his career as that of a typical British officer.

In April 1796 the Thirty-third was embarked for India, whither Wellesley was at the moment too ill to accompany it. He overtook it, however, at the Cape in a fast-sailing frigate, having meanwhile been promoted colonel on the 3rd of May, and landed with it at Calcutta in February 1797. By this time he had given up both fiddling and card-playing, and was devoting several hours a day to serious study, having, it is likely enough, acquired the habit during the long and tedious voyage to India. It is evident from a letter which he wrote in April 1797, on the subject of light artillery, that he had carefully studied former Indian campaigns; and it may have been the ability and knowledge, displayed in this and similar official documents, which procured for him the command of a small expedition of about fifteen hundred men which was sent from Bengal with the design of attacking Batavia and Manila. Another contingent was to sail from Madras, and the selected Commander-in-Chief was a man of known incapacity, whose shortcomings were to be made good by a competent staff. Wellesley, not perhaps without recollection of the Duke of York, condemned the arrangement. "A good high-spirited army," he wrote, "cannot be kept in order by other means than the abilities and firmness of the Commander-in-Chief." He quarrelled further, quite rightly, with the medical arrangements, which took out of his hands the control and management of the sick, once again recalling the awful condition of the medical staff in the Low Countries. He drew up a routine of duties for his men in the transports, specially prescribing daily exercise with dumb-bells, and he fought a successful battle with the captains of the East Indiamen for the right of retaining command of his own men on board ship. In fact, this young colonel of eight-and-twenty claimed to look after his soldiers himself, whether in sickness or in health, whatever might have been the practice in former East Indian campaigns; and he had his way. He was not violent nor unconciliatory, but he was very firm, for he cared for his men.

After all, the expedition against Manila came to naught, being recalled when it had reached Penang; but Wellesley did not fail to represent to the authorities the strategetic value of Penang and the means of holding it, with a small force, against all enemies. On his return he drew up an elaborate memorandum upon the state and commerce of

Bengal, showing that he took as much interest in social and economic as in military questions; and then he addressed himself once more to wider matters of diplomatic and military policy. His eldest brother, Lord Mornington, arrived in India as Governor-General in May 1798, and in him Arthur knew that he had an able chief who would both listen and understand. The condition of British India was at the moment most perilous. Weak and bad administration had brought low the credit of the Government, impaired the discipline of the armies, and destroyed all efficiency in the military departments. Englishmen had by no means yet shaken off the tradition that India existed chiefly for them to make money out of. Corruption was deeply rooted in all branches of civil and military service; and both governors of presidencies and generals, sent out from England, thought less of their duty than of filling their pockets by means which, though not discountenanced by any authority, were none the less discreditable. High position, moreover, was specially valued in India, as in England, for the patronage that it carried with it; and the civil governors, true to their political training at home, were particularly rapacious of patronage. It was therefore their practice to arrogate to themselves the right of bestowing all military as well as all civil appointments; and the generals, caring little so long as they accumulated their handsome emoluments, submitted without a protest. The result was that the military service was utterly disorganised. Fortresses were unrepaired, magazines left empty, the auxiliary departments allowed to go to ruin. Officers had no encouragement to gain the approval of their military superiors, and readily succumbed to the climatic influence which tempted them to idleness. Above all, their discipline was seriously impaired. They owed no allegiance to the King, being the servants of the East India Company, for which they felt no respect, and from which they could look for no honour. Hence, as Arthur Wellesley at once perceived, the officers of the native army, especially in Bengal, were a corporate body, clinging closely together, whose discontent was therefore more dangerous than in other armies. His fears were realised within eleven years by the officers' mutiny of 1809.

Yet, amid all this apathy and neglect, the dominance of England in India had never been more seriously threatened. The French were intriguing with sundry of the native potentates for the overthrow of their old rivals, and French officers were busy casting guns and training troops alike for Tipu Sahib, sovereign of Mysore, for the Nizam of Hyderabad, and for the most powerful and ambitious of the Mahratta chiefs, Madaji Scindia. The most dangerous of these was the first named, Tipu Sahib, who, like his father, Hyder Ali, before him, had made many a descent upon the Carnatic, bringing famine to tens of thousands by plunder and devastation.   There were good and reasonable grounds enough for declaration of war against Tipu; but a march to his capital, Seringapatam, as hard experience had proved, was no light matter. Tipu, following the example of his father, had imitated the English in establishing regular infantry trained by European officers, and providing himself with a vast number of guns cast by European founders.   Herein he had followed a false policy, for he could never hope to raise his troops to the perfection attained by the British and the East India Company's sepoys; and, meanwhile, he neglected the true source of his strength—his light cavalry, ubiquitous yet elusive and impossible to bring to action, which destroyed all the forage in front of an invading enemy, and never ceased to harry his flanks and rear.   Cornwallis had suffered cruelly from them during his advance upon Seringapatam in 1791, and had been driven back in ignominious and costly retreat. He had made good his failure and stormed Seringapatam in 1792, but with great effort and at great expense. Remembering this, Arthur Wellesley counselled that, whatever the provocation given by Tipu, hostilities should be deferred until it was absolutely certain that he could be disposed of in a single campaign. Meanwhile he pointed out that the best way of checking any raid upon the Carnatic was a counter-invasion of Mysore, and he advocated the immediate establishment of advanced bases, with supplies, munitions, and stores, and above all, the collection of sufficient transport. Though no more than a colonel of a battalion of the line, he practically took upon himself the functions of chief of the general staff to his brother, the Governor-General.

At the beginning of 1798 Arthur Wellesley paid a visit to Lord Hobart, the Governor of Madras, who was an old acquaintance, and spent two profitable months in making an exhaustive study of the resources and condition of that presidency. In August he was sent with his regiment from Calcutta to Madras, nominally only as commanding officer of his battalion, but really as the Governor-General's agent, to explain and forward his views and his military preparations. Meanwhile, acting always upon his brother's advice, Mornington, by a judicious mixture of persuasion and menace, recalled the Nizam to his old friendship, disarmed his French troops, and gained the use of his trained infantry for the British. He then approached Scindia and succeeded in obtaining from him a promise of neutrality in case of war with Mysore. Thus the ground was cleared, at any rate for a time, of all enemies but Tipu Sahib.

To the end of the year Arthur Wellesley worked quietly but strenuously at the preparations for a possible campaign. The treasury at Madras was empty, the Governor was nervous and stupid, the Council lacked backbone, the Military Board, which managed military affairs with extreme inefficiency, was obstructive and suspicious. The General, George Harris, a veteran of the American War, alone stood by him and invited his advice; but Harris was diffident and disinclined to assert himself, his predecessors having been deprived of all power by successive Governors of Madras. Arthur Wellesley, however, to use his own words, "lectured him well" on these shortcomings, rallied the Madras Army to his support, and wrestled indefatigably against the powers of jealousy and imbecility to collect bullocks and grain, accumulate supplies and stores, and stir up energy among the most apathetic. Money was so scarce that he actually had to borrow from his officers and to sell his own horses in order to get two detachments of troops to their destination. He even summoned his brother, the Governor-General, to Madras that his energy and presence might hasten matters forward. In January 1799 he still advocated gentleness with Tipu, thinking the preparations to be still insufficiently perfect; but Mornington judged otherwise, and in February ordered General Harris to take command and invade Mysore, proposing further to accompany the army in person. "If I were in General Harris's situation, and the Governor-General were to join the army, I should quit it," wrote Arthur to his august brother. Mornington decided to stay at Madras.

The army, about twenty thousand strong, had been concentrated at Vellore, about ninety miles, as the crow flies, west and south of Madras, and one hundred and eighty miles from the objective, Seringapatam. It was joined, after a march or two, by the Nizam's contingent of about sixteen

thousand men, ten thousand of them regular disciplined troops; and, since their selected commander had managed to get himself killed in a duel,
the Thirty-third was added to them, and Arthur
Wellesley was placed in command of the whole.
In co-operation with these thirty-six thousand men,
a contingent of six thousand men from Bombay,
under General Stuart, was to land at Cannanore
and close in upon Seringapatam from the west.
Tipu Sahib's force was reckoned at thirty-three
thousand infantry, besides fifteen thousand cavalry
and rocket-men; and he had the advantage of
operating upon interior lines.

Arthur Wellesley described the army as a ponderous machine, and so it was. "In India," he
once wrote, "armies take the field with arsenals
and magazines, which they always carry with
them"; and the force might as conveniently have
been concentrated at Madras as at the forward post
of Vellore. The advance was made in two columns, the British force on the right, the Nizam's
contingent on the left, which with cavalry thrown
out to front and rear made a hollow square, having
a front of about three miles and a depth of about
seven. Within it was a moving city, containing
about one hundred and fifty thousand followers,

about one hundred and twenty thousand bullocks
—more than half of them latter private property,
for Indian officers liked to do their fighting com-
fortably—and elephants and camels and horses and
asses, in fact, a confusion of trumpeting and squeal-
ing and braying and lowing, mingled with the yells
of men, the chatter of women, and the crying of children. Of course this vast concourse of animals
needed food, and Tipu's cavalry was on the watch
to lay the country waste on the line of its advance;
so that Harris was obliged to pursue a zigzag
course, taking any direction in which forage was to
be found. Even thus the cattle began to fail
very early; great quantities of ammunition were
abandoned; and matters began to look so serious
ten days after the army entered Mysore that an
inquiry was held, when it was found that the
Commissariat-bullocks were being starved to death
in strict accordance with regulation. The regula-
tions were altered; some superfluous stores, which
Wellesley had begged Harris to leave behind, were
destroyed; and things were a little improved.
Incredible though it may seem, the force managed
to traverse ten or twelve miles, sometimes even
twenty, in a day; but, as Arthur Wellesley observed, if Tipu had handled his troops, and in

particular his light cavalry, with proper skill, progress would have been very much slower and would probably have been arrested altogether.

To do Tipu justice, he made a bold attempt to overwhelm the Bombay force before it could join Harris, but he failed. He failed also to stop the advance of Harris in a general action five and twenty miles east of Seringapatam, though his infantry fought bravely and stood firm till the Thirty-third had almost closed upon them with the bayonet. On the 5th of April Harris's army sat down before Seringapatam, and on that same evening Wellesley was ordered to clear a grove of trees, known as the Sultanpettah Tope, which was held by the enemy as an outlying post about three thousand yards south of the walls. He entered it accordingly at the head of the flank companies of the Thirty-third, in the blackness of an intensely dark night. He was received by a sharp fire in front and flanks; the two companies ran away; the rest of the battalion, which was in support, lost itself in the darkness; and Wellesley returned in much agitation to report his misfortune to Harris. He made his failure good on the morrow, and a few days later he wrote to his brother an account of the matter with perfect calmness. "But," he

added, "I have come to a determination, when in
my power, never to suffer an attack to be made by
night upon an enemy who is prepared and strongly
posted, and whose posts have not been recon-
noitred by daylight." Thus he learned his lesson;
but it is none the less certain that he was more
than usually mortified by his failure. "Wellesley
is mad," is the significant entry in a brother officer's
journal. In fact, this is the one recorded occasion
when Arthur Wellesley showed signs of being
flustered.

The siege proceeded without any further occasion
for prominent action upon his part, though not
without provoking his indignation over the squan-
dering of the supplies which he had been so inde-
fatigable in collecting before the campaign. On
the 26th of April Seringapatam was stormed, and
for a week the troops and followers gave themselves up to plunder. At last on the 5th of May
Arthur Wellesley was appointed to the command
of the place, when by ruthless hanging and flogging
he restored order among the troops and confidence
among the inhabitants. From beginning to end
of his life he abhorred above all things anarchy and
oppression; and an army out of hand is the most
ruthless of oppressors. Rapidly and surely he

made his arrangements for the administration of justice within the city, in his leisure moments writing to his brother his views as to the future of Mysore. The disbanding of Tipu's army, meanwhile, turned loose a number of desperate men upon the country who found a leader in an old freebooter, named Dundia Wao, and under his guidance ravaged and plundered with merciless greed and cruelty. Two flying columns sent after them in July succeeded in dispersing two bands of these ruffians; and in the third week of August Harris with the bulk of the army returned to Madras, leaving Arthur Wellesley in full military and civil command of Mysore.

Administrative business called him first to the north, but the entire country was disturbed, and bodies of banditti were roving in all directions. On his return to Seringapatam he took measures to deal with two of the most troublesome of these gangs, his orders to that end being very terse and pithy. "There is a place called Ey Goor, four or five coss from Munserabad," he wrote to a captain of the Seventy-fourth. "You will be pleased to destroy it, and hang all persons either in it or in Munserabad that you find in arms." Then in April Dundia Wao reappeared, more formidable than ever, defeated a body of Mahratta horse that had been sent against him, and, accumulating the riff-raff of the country about him as he advanced, was soon at the head of forty thousand men. It was necessary for the Colonel himself to take the field, with five regiments of horse and seven battalions of foot (two of each being British) under his personal command, and with another column of about half that strength in co-operation with him.

The problem set to him was to exterminate an enemy who held a few strong native fortresses as bases, but kept the bulk of his force moving with extreme rapidity, and sedulously avoided a general action. The fortresses would present little or no difficulty, for experience taught that, if once British troops gained a footing in any Indian stronghold, resistance collapsed at once. But to hunt down bodies of elusive men, for the most part mounted, demanded swift marching and, to that end, very efficient transport. Wellesley had urged again and again the expediency of maintaining an establishment of draft-bullocks and a corps of disciplined bullock-drivers both for the guns and for the transport of the army, for he had observed that the drivers of hired cattle always neglected their beasts and, no matter what the abundance of forage, allowed them to starve.   He spoke to deaf ears; the Military Board, which controlled matters at Madras, being far too stupid and corrupt to change their old-fashioned and inefficient methods.   The result justified his prescience.   He started on his campaign in the middle of June, and after a month spent in storming fortresses and making long marches, was obliged to halt for two days to replenish supplies and stores.   Those two days cost him half of his cattle, for the drivers refused to take them out two or three miles to graze; and a spell of severe weather, catching them weakened by starvation, killed them off by thousands.

None the less he made good his losses somehow and continued to follow up Dundia, striking him hard but not decisive blows, until his power was so much weakened that Wellesley decided to break up his own force into three columns and to use at least one of them to head the enemy, while the others pursued.   At last on the 10th of September he in person at the head of four regiments of horse overtook Dundia, who fell back to a strong position with the five thousand men that were with him. Wellesley formed his four regiments into a single line, charged at their head, and swept the five thousand to the four winds.   Dundia was killed;

the remnant of his followers was easily hunted down, and the country was delivered from the curse of his oppression. It was the first and last occasion on which Wellesley led a charge of cavalry; and there can be little doubt that he thoroughly enjoyed it.

So ended his first essay in independent command, a small enterprise no doubt, but not by any means an easy one. There had been one such campaign before—that of Tarleton in Carolina in 1780—and there have been several since, as, for instance, the hunting down of Baji Rao in 1818, of Chitu in 1819, of Tantia Topi in 1858, and, in its later stages, during the South African War of 1899–1901. They signify long marches, with extreme fatigue and privation to the troops, which often end in disappointment and failure; and the trial to their patience and endurance is consequently very severe. Much, therefore, depends upon their confidence in their commander, who, in his turn, is in a most difficult position, compelled to make great demands upon his men, and frequently, through the impossibility of obtaining good intelligence, unable to give them speedy success in return. Wellesley was more severely tried than most of his kind owing to the slackness and incompetence of the Madras

Commissariat. Their dilatoriness, for instance, caused him to reach the river Werda just twenty-four hours after it had risen in deep flood, and delayed him for ten days before he could cross. But indeed when it required from eight to ten different military departments to provide five thousand men with transport, as was the case at Madras, it is not surprising that their subordinate officers in outlying stations frequently failed. Close study of original documents is necessary to realise how rotten was the whole system of Indian administration, not merely in 1800, but fifty years later.

In May, when preparing for the campaign against Dundia, Wellesley received the offer to command yet another expedition which was projected against Batavia. He was much tempted to accept it, but forbore to do so until he had ascertained the wishes of Lord Clive, the Governor of Madras. Clive was filled with dismay at the prospect of losing his services in Mysore. Colonel Barry Close, whom Wellesley described as by far the ablest man in the East India's Company's army, added his remonstrances to Clive's; and the Governor-General withdrew the offer, adding the graceful compliment, "Your conduct in Mysore has secured you character and advancement for the remainder of your life." Wellesley continued, therefore, to apply himself to the pacification of Mysore.

So matters went on until November 1800, when he received orders to proceed to Trincomalee and take command of a force of about four thousand men for an expedition to Mauritius. The Governor-General had been apprised of Bonaparte's landing in Egypt and of his designs against India, and wished to safeguard himself against them by seizing France's chief naval base in East Indian waters. After drawing up an exact account of all the pacificatory operations which he was projecting for his successor in Mysore, Arthur Wellesley made his way to the west coast and arrived at Trincomalee about Christmas 1800. The Governor of Ceylon was undone to know the destination of the armament; "But," wrote Wellesley to his brother with the biting humour which was characteristic of him, "I don't recommend that he should be informed of the object of the expedition until the disclosure of it to all India is not likely to be prejudicial to the operations which are to be carried into execution." Then came another complication. The British Government announced its intention of attacking the French in Egypt not only from the west but from the east. For the first time troops were to converge upon a single objective from both of the great military bases of the Empire, the British Isles and India, a very memorable event which a happier fate might have bound up with the name of Arthur Wellesley.

But it was not to be. The armament was now to be increased to a strength which required a general officer to take command, and Arthur Wellesley was but a colonel, whereas Sir David Baird was a major-general of two years' standing. Mornington judged that, in such circumstances, his brother would not wish to serve in Egypt, though he seems to have been sanguine that Arthur might yet have time to capture Mauritius before the expedition should sail for the Red Sea. Arthur, however, though fully sharing his brother's opinion that he would be useless under the command of Baird or of Sir James Craig, who had also been named by Mornington, looked more deeply into the heart of things. Mornington's next design, forced upon him by the Admiral on the station, was to give up the attack on Mauritius and resume his former enterprise against Batavia, appointing Baird to the chief command and Arthur Wellesley as second.

This left Arthur unmoved. He realised that co-operation with the British Army in Egypt was the first duty of his force; and, after consultation with the senior naval officer at Trincomalee, he carried it, without orders and upon his own responsibility, to Bombay. Herein, undoubtedly, he acted in the spirit of the Cabinet's instructions from England; but the step was a very bold one for a mere colonel to take; and Mornington, as well as the Governor of Ceylon, called him somewhat sternly to account for it. Arthur defended himself with his usual direct common sense; and, since fresh and urgent instructions as to the Egyptian expedition proved him to be right, Mornington approved his conduct in the actual circumstances of the case, while condemning it in the abstract as likely to establish an inconvenient precedent. The incident furnishes rather a striking comment on the characters of the two brothers. Both were very able, both very masterful; but, while Mornington was so intent upon his own minor projects that he could see little beyond them, Arthur, though he had everything to gain from seconding his brother in executing those projects for him, took a broader and keener view. He realised at once that operations against Dutch and French settlements in

East Indian waters were as naught in comparison with driving the French from Egypt and securing the shortest line of communication between England and India.

On the voyage, and while at Bombay, he laboured strenuously to work out every detail of Baird's task for him; but in April he fell sick of fever and other disorders, and decided that he could not accompany the expedition. He parted with Baird, who had been very jealous of him ever since his appointment to command the Nizam's contingent before Seringapatam, on the most friendly terms; the difficult and rather cantankerous old Scot showing a genuine desire that Wellesley should accompany him. But Arthur's general feeling was that he had been ill-used, and the more so since, when first appointed to the command of the force at Trincomalee, he had been told to select his own staff, and was now obliged to disappoint some of his best and most promising young officers. However, as he remarked, a man who could not sacrifice his private views to public spirit was worth very little; and he confessed that the past five months had been the most interesting of his life. So Baird sailed to the Red Sea without him, crossed the desert from Casseir to Keneh, and reached the Nile to find that Abercromby and Hutchinson had already victoriously accomplished the work of the Egyptian campaign.

By the end of April Wellesley had returned to his command in Mysore, where he took up the reins with all his old activity, though not yet free from intermittent fever. "I know but one receipt for good health in this country," he wrote to his brother Henry, in July, "and that is to live moderately, to drink little or no wine, to use exercise, to keep the mind employed, and, if possible, to keep in good humour with the world. The last is the most difficult, for, as you have often observed, there is hardly a good-tempered man in India." There is no reason to suppose that Arthur Wellesley was ever much given to eating or drinking, for his palate was singularly insensitive. He could not distinguish fresh butter from rancid, nor sound wine from sour. But it is reasonable to assign the extreme abstemiousness, which distinguished him to the end of his life, to this period of his rule in Mysore, where he saw white men falling down all round him owing to drink, idleness, or sloth. Though Seringapatam, his headquarters, was extremely unhealthy, he seems to have suffered little from the climate there himself. But then, to use his own expression, he "used exercise," riding far and wide all over the province to see things with his own eyes. Also, he certainly kept his mind occupied. Every item of administration came up before him for settlement, and not one was shirked. There were financial questions, such as the rate of exchange and the remedies against debased coinage, and highly technical matters, such as road-making, bridge-building, timber-felling, construction of barracks, all of them additional to the administrative routine of meting out justice and punishing crime. There were nests of robbers, European as well as native, military as well as civil, to be harried and destroyed, not always with encouragement either from the Military Board at Madras or from the Board of East India Directors at home. There were endless quarrels between drunken officers to be composed, and constant brutality of bad officers towards the natives to be suppressed; and amid all these difficulties there was the population of a conquered territory to be protected and conciliated, and its garrison to be maintained in good behaviour, good health and efficiency. There were the bad traditions of half a century to be effaced, if possible, among the British in India, military neglect one of the worst

of them.   One of the few occasions in which we see
Arthur Wellesley's wrath blazing out at white heat
is when a careless colonel allows a detachment of his
battalion to be surrounded and cut to pieces, and
then, in abject terror, gathers the rest of his men
into a fort and sits there on the defensive.   Against
this host of evils, moral and military, he battled
unceasingly sometimes by punishment, more often
by precept, and ever and always by example.   For
he was not content merely to put down that which
was wrong; he strove unceasingly to exalt the
right, and to raise the standard of duty and integrity.   And he brought to the task the mightiest
strength that can reinforce an indomitable will—
clean hands and a clean heart.

In January 1802 he was again called into the field
in person to subdue the Raja of Balam, on the
western border of Mysore, who was in rebellion.
The enterprise was a troublesome one, for the
scene of operations was a narrow tract of jungle in
which mishaps were easily encountered and the
enemy could only with difficulty be brought to
action.   He had laid down the principle that, in
such a campaign, the troops must move slowly,
clearing away the growth for some distance on
either side of every track, so as to deprive the

enemy of their great source of strength—the means
of concealment. But even so he despaired of laying hands on the leader, who was the fountain of
all mischief. However, dividing his force into
three columns, he ordered them to converge at a
given time upon a certain village stronghold in the
forest. Two of them, which had started from
exactly opposite directions, reached the village at
the same moment, and the third was not far behind. The place, which had foiled an attack made
by troops under other commanders some months
before, was carried with little loss; and then began the weary pursuit of the Raja. The whole
country was covered with thick short jungle, and no
intelligence concerning him was procurable. "I
don't think I ever saw a country naturally so
strong as this," Wellesley wrote, "and to the
strength of which so many additions have been
made by the natives themselves. Every village is
a strong fortification, of which it would require
good troops to take possession; and in some cases
ten or a dozen of these villages are connected by
made or natural defences of great strength." He
therefore proposed a condition for sparing the inhabitants, that they should themselves destroy these
formidable defences; and, gaining their confidence,

[51]

he was able to drive their leader from the jungle and capture him within three weeks after his first successful attack. The Raja and six other principal rebels were hanged, and Balam was reduced to submission and obedience. The ease with which this task was accomplished has obscured its vast difficulties, which were only overcome by sound foresight, endless care, and unsleeping vigilance; and these little campaigns were rich in training and experience for the more serious work that was close at hand.

The destruction of Tipu Sahib's power had at last brought the British in India face to face with the rival power of Mahrattas, who, but for the unlooked for intervention of Europeans in Indian affairs, would undoubtedly have become masters of the whole peninsula. The Mahratta Confederacy,[1] however, was at this time in confusion owing to the jealous rivalry of its members; and Mornington, who would gladly have lived at peace with them, was unable to do so because its nominal chief, the Peishwa, could not enforce the observance of any treaty upon his subordinates. A series of

---

[1] It may be well to recall to readers the members of the Mahratta Confederacy—Peishwa of Poona, Gaikwar of Baroda, Scindia of Gwalior, Bhonsla of Nagpur, Holkar of Indore.

combats between Holkar of Indore on the one hand, and the Peishwa and Scindia of Gwalior on the other, had resulted by the end of 1802 in the flight of the Peishwa and an appeal from him for the protection of the British Government. This was granted by the compact of offensive and defensive alliance called the Treaty of Bassein, which was signed on the 31st of December 1802; and Mornington at once ordered the assembly of a powerful force at Harihar on the northern border of Mysore, adjoining the Peishwa's dominions, with the double object of repelling any possible invasion by hostile Mahrattas and of escorting the Peishwa to his capital at Poona.

This force was entrusted to Arthur Wellesley, upon whom fell the whole burden of the preparations for its advance. As usual his chief care was for transport and supply. If he could feed his troops there would be no excuse for plunder or marauding; the inhabitants of the territory through which he passed, being unoppressed, would not be unfriendly; and, above all, strict discipline could be preserved. Among the most valuable of the captures from Tipu Sahib was his stud of draft-bullocks, the famous bullocks of Mysore, which can walk four miles and trot six miles an hour;

and Arthur Wellesley had kept a jealous eye upon them from the first, for, above all men, he appreciated their worth to a British Army. There was to be no more trailing about in a huge hollow square with a moving city in the midst of it. All baggage was to be cut down to the smallest compass, and all followers reduced to the lowest figure. "The only mode," he wrote, "in which we can inspire either our enemies or our allies with respect for our operations will be to show them that the army can move with ease and celerity at all times and in all situations."

All being ready, he crossed the Toombuddra into Mahratta territory on the 12th of March 1803, Holkar steadily retreating before him. By the 1st of April he had passed the Kistna, one hundred and twenty miles to north, with his cattle still in perfect condition. On the 19th, hearing that Holkar had himself retreated far to north of Poona, but had left a small force there to plunder and destroy it, Arthur Wellesley rode on with his cavalry only, and, traversing sixty-two miles in thirty hours, arrived on the 20th to find that the enemy had fled and that Poona was safe. The Peishwa re-entered his capital on the 15th of May, and all seemed to be well.

But meanwhile new trouble had appeared. Under the Treaty of Amiens, which in March 1802 gave a short truce to the war between England and France, it had been stipulated that the French possessions in India should be restored to them; and Bonaparte had sent out an able French officer to take them over, with secret instructions to think out the means of carrying on war against the British there. Now came warning from the British Government that hostilities in Europe were likely to be renewed, and that the restoration of the captured possessions must be delayed. Such a prospect was not likely to foster a pacific spirit in Scindia. He had been in correspondence with the French Directory; his troops were trained and commanded by French officers; and he saw visions of succeeding to the position of the Mogul Emperors. He, therefore, made endless pretexts for refusing acceptance of the Treaty of Bassein, and insisted that Bhonsla, another leading member of the Confederacy, must come to discuss it with him. Bhonsla came on the 3rd of June, bringing with him his whole army for escort; but still the Governor-General was patient. Scindia and Bhonsla continued to play the game of procrastination, spending the time in endeavouring to per-

[55]

suade Holkar to join them. Nevertheless Mornington was loth to precipitate hostilities, until at last on the 3rd of August his patience broke down, and the issue was committed to the hazard of war.

Arthur Wellesley's indignation over all this delay was extreme. He understood the tactics of the Mahrattas. They, even as Tipu, had been tempted to follow the British model, to organise infantry and cast vast quantities of cannon under the teaching of European officers, whereas they had better have stuck to the guerilla bands and tactics of their first great leader, Sivaji. But Wellesley had taken note of their ways. They avoided decisive engagements unless they could accept battle in a strong position, which they always chose and occupied with great skill, so as to make the most of their very numerous and powerful artillery; and, so far as their military reforms permitted, they still clung to their old principles of harassing rather than meeting an enemy. The problem was how to catch them and force them to fight on ground that was not of their choosing. Arthur Wellesley solved it by preparing his campaign for the rainy season, when the rivers would be full. He had many months earlier asked for boats and pontoons from Bombay, so that he might be able to cross any river, whereas the Mahrattas, being dependent on fords, would be stopped by any flood. With this and the further advantage of a well-organised transport and supply-service he felt confident that he could follow his elusive enemy so rapidly that he could be sure of overtaking them and attacking them at their disadvantage. No matter how strong a position the Mahrattas might occupy, they could not stay there long because they lived on the country, whereas he could sit down opposite to them for an indefinite time. He could have his food brought to him; the Mahrattas would never dare to assail him; and he had only to wait for them to move off in order to fall upon them on the march.

The prolonged tolerance of Mornington frustrated Arthur Wellesley's plans, so far as the rainy season was concerned; and the obstruction of the Bombay Government brought other details of it to naught. Recognising that his nominal base at Seringapatam, being five hundred miles away, was inconveniently remote, Wellesley had arranged for the formation of a large depot on the coast, within easy reach of Bombay by sea and of easy access to Poona by land; and the Bombay Government had promised to send thither bullocks to drag supplies from the depot to the camp. Not a bullock arrived. The

Bombay Government had also promised to send pontoons; but contrived to put them on carriages which broke down after one day's march. By June Wellesley gave up the Bombay Government in despair, and looked about to fend for himself. The joint forces of Scindia and Bhonsla lay about the Ajanta pass, roughly two hundred miles, as the crow flies, northeast of Poona. On the way, some eighty miles from Poona, stood the fort of Ahmednagar, which struck him as well suited for an advanced base, the more so since, as he said, the whole property of the country was lodged there, under the protection of about a thousand regular soldiers and as many Arabs of Scindia's army. In July he shifted his camp to within eight miles of Ahmednagar, and awaited the moment when he should be slipped from the leash.

His army was now some eleven thousand strong, including over sixteen hundred Europeans, besides some five thousand irregular native horse, with fourteen field-pieces and eight light horse-artillery guns. Working in co-operation with him was the contingent of the Nizam of Hyderabad, about nine thousand strong, the great bulk of them regular native troops of the Company's army, but including nine hundred Europeans of the Regular army.

[58]

This force, commanded by Colonel Stevenson, was guarding the passes of the Nizam's northern frontier about Aurungabad, some seventy miles north of Wellesley's camp. Yet another fifty miles to north, about the Ajanta pass, lay the joint forces of Bhonsla and Scindia, ten thousand five hundred regular infantry, a thousand matchlock-men and rocket-men, and thirty-eight thousand cavalry, with one hundred and ninety guns.

On the 6th of August Wellesley received news of the final rupture of negotiations; on the 7th he was unable to move owing to foul weather; but on the 8th he made a spring upon the fortified town beneath the fortress of Ahmednagar, and carried it by escalade with inconsiderable loss. "These Englishmen are strange people, and their general is a wonderful man," wrote a Mahratta chief from Wellesley's camp after the action. "They came here in the morning, looked at the wall, walked over it, killed all the garrison, and returned to breakfast." Four days more sufficed for the reduction of the fortress itself, and Wellesley thus secured not only his advanced base but a strong post that covered both Poona and the Nizam's western frontier. Yet another four days were occupied in arranging for the protection and government of the conquered territory, and then the march northward was resumed, and by the 29th of August he was at Aurungabad. It is noteworthy that, since the Bombay Government had failed to provide him with pontoons, he had set his troops to make boats of wickerwork which were then covered with bullock-skins; and on these he crossed the great river Godavari, though it was in heavy flood.

In the interval the enemy had kept Stevenson, who was a nervous man, in a state of miserable tension by making a feint to eastward, and then shifting westward and moving south-westward as if to advance upon Hyderabad. But upon Wellesley's arrival the Mahrattas withdrew again to Ajanta, and, finally, on the 21st of September, took up a position about twenty miles to south of it, at Assaye on the river Kaitna. On that day Wellesley and Stevenson met at Badnauoor, about twenty miles south of the Kaitna, and Wellesley determined that he and Stevenson should converge upon the enemy by two different routes, nearly fifteen miles apart, and attack him on the evening of the 24th. It was a dangerous game to play, for it gave the Mahratta chiefs the chance of throwing their whole strength upon either moiety of the force before their junction; but Wellesley was anxious to save time, and, knowing that his enemy was afraid of him, did not hesitate to take liberties.

On the 23rd he arrived within six miles of the Kaitna, where he heard that the Mahratta cavalry had withdrawn, but that the infantry was standing fast. He resolved to attack them at once, sent a message to inform Stevenson accordingly, and set his force in motion, riding forward himself with his cavalry and his staff. At one o'clock he came in sight not of the Mahratta infantry only but of the entire army, fifty thousand strong, strongly posted on a peninsula between two rivers, namely, the Kaitna in their front, impassable except by certain fords, and the Juah, of less volume but with very steep banks, in their rear; the junction of the two streams covering their left flank. This was highly disconcerting. Wellesley had made it his rule never to attack Mahrattas in a position of their own choosing; but the least sign of retiring would have brought the Mahratta cavalry buzzing round the column of march like a swarm of bees, and exposed him to deadly peril. Moreover, it was his principle never to retreat before Orientals. Though his men had already marched twenty-four miles, there was nothing for it but to attack; but the trouble was that his guides knew of but one ford over the Kaitna, and it could be seen that this was commanded by the Mahratta batteries. Observing, however, two villages over against each other on opposite sides of the river, he concluded that there must be a ford between them, and he proved to be right. By that ford, therefore, he ordered his army to cross into the peninsula, reckoning that at least he could attack his enemy in flank, since they could not possibly possess sufficient skill in manœuvre to change front.

Here again he miscalculated. The Mahrattas foolishly made no attempt to impede his passage of the river, but they did change front with regularity and order; and, when Wellesley formed his order of battle, he found the enemy facing him, with their right flank protected by the Kaitna and their left not by the Juah only but by the fortified village of Assaye, while a hundred guns, admirably served, along a front of less than a mile opened a heavy and very destructive fire.

No troops could long endure this, and Wellesley gave the order to advance, himself leading the left wing in person, and instructing Colonel Orrock, who commanded on the right, on no account to attack Assaye, nor even to approach too close to it.

On the left Wellesley's wing charged up to the Mahratta batteries with the bayonet; and, though the gunners stood most gallantly till they were killed at their posts, the Mahratta infantry in rear of them gave way at once. On the right, Orrock, through some blunder, led his men straight upon Assaye, where they lost so heavily that the Sepoys gave way; and, but for the heroic conduct of the Seventy-fourth and an opportune charge of the Nineteenth Light Dragoons, matters would have been serious. The enemy's right, thrust back by Wellesley, reformed with its back to the Juah, aligning itself upon the defenders of Assaye and the Mahratta reserve, at right angles to the original front; and had the Mahratta leaders possessed any courage they might still have overwhelmed Wellesley when he wheeled up his left wing to attack them. But they mistrusted themselves, and their men mistrusted them; and the Mahratta host after five hours of desperate combat broke up and moved off the field, leaving twelve hundred dead and ninety-eight guns behind them.

So severe an engagement had never before been fought by the British in India. Wellesley's casualties amounted to nearly fifteen hundred, of whom six hundred and fifty were Europeans. The

WELLINGTON

Seventy-fourth was almost annihilated, every officer being killed or wounded, and nearly four hundred out of fewer than five hundred men. In fact, the day was won only by the most heroic exertions of all ranks,[1] and at its close all were utterly exhausted. Arthur Wellesley throughout the fight had always been at hand where most wanted, perfectly calm, cool, and collected. Two horses were killed under him, and eight out of ten of his staff sustained wounds to themselves or their horses; but he escaped unhurt. Night came down gloomily upon the victorious host, all being too weary to do more than throw themselves on the ground. The dead were ungathered, the wounded, for the most part horribly shattered by cannon-shot, were in many cases unattended. The living lay down among the dead, and Wellesley sank down with the rest. On one side of him was an officer whose leg had been shot away, on the other a second officer, dead; and he sat there motionless, with his head bent low between his knees and spoke not a word. Never again till Waterloo was an army under his

---

[1] One officer of the Nineteenth Light Dragoons, who had lost one arm and accidentally broken the wrist of the other, charged with his bridle in his teeth and his sword in his injured hand. This shows the spirit of Wellesley's officers; and there were other examples of hardly less heroism.

command to stand in such peril, nor owe its victory
so completely to the tenacity of his will.

On the evening of the next day Stevenson arrived
and took up the pursuit, but the Mahrattas never
paused until they reached Ajanta. By the middle
of October, Wellesley had mastered the whole of
Scindia's dominions in the Deccan, and on the
11th of November emissaries arrived from that
chief to sue for peace. Wellesley named his conditions, which Scindia made no attempt to fulfil,
but sent his infantry north to be out of harm's
way, and with his cavalry struck east to rejoin his
ally, Bhonsla. Wellesley followed him up, and on
the 24th of November at the end of a long march
perceived from the top of a tower a confused mass
in motion about five miles away. Though his
troops had been on foot for nine hours, he set them
on the march at once and came up with the enemy
drawn up in order of battle about eight miles
north-east of Ajanta, at Argaum.

He attacked forthwith, but the action opened
badly with a panic among the three leading battalions of Sepoys, while he was forming his array for
battle. Happily, being on the spot himself, he
speedily restored order. The Mahrattas, though
thirty to forty thousand strong, made a poor re-

sistance, and soon ran, leaving thirty-eight guns behind them. Wellesley promptly sent in pursuit his cavalry, which cut down three thousand of the fugitives and captured vast trains of animals and huge quantities of baggage. Yet the initial panic had been very perilous. "I am convinced," he wrote, "that, if I had not been near to rally the Sepoys and restore the battle, we should have lost the day."

The defeated Mahrattas took refuge in the fort of Gawilghur, some fifty miles to north-east of Argaum, and Wellesley arrived before it on the 6th of December. The place lay among rocky mountains, so difficult of access that only with the greatest difficulty was heavy artillery brought into position; and its defences both natural and artificial were most formidable. Stevenson nominally took charge of the siege while Wellesley covered his operations; but, Stevenson being old and infirm, Wellesley did the work of both, which signified a daily ride of fifty miles. The batteries opened fire on the 12th; the assault was delivered from two sides simultaneously by Stevenson's and Wellesley's troops on the 15th; the outer fort, citadel, and inner citadel were mastered with astonishingly little difficulty, and in a few hours Gawilghur was in Wellesley's possession. On the following day Bhonsla sent in emissaries to sue for peace; and on the 17th a treaty was signed, whereby he yielded sundry territories to the East India Company and its allies. Thus one member of the Mahratta Confederacy had been vanquished, and Wellesley's work in the field was practically done. One more effort was required of him in February through the appearance of a gang of banditti on the Nizam's borders. Taking a detachment of horse and foot he started at 6 A. M. on the 4th of February, halted from noon till 10 P.M., resumed his march and overtook and destroyed his enemy at noon on the 5th, having traversed sixty miles in thirty hours. This was the last military enterprise conducted by him in India.

Of the other operations conducted against the Mahrattas farther north by General Gerard Lake, with many brilliant successes, but not without undue share of reverses and even of disgrace, Wellesley knew little more than any other high official in India. But more than once he predicted the disasters that must inevitably follow upon certain lines of conduct, and did his utmost by wise counsel, though in vain, to avert them. Nor did he spare sharp criticism of junior officers, notably of one Colonel John Murray, whose incorrigible feebleness and irresolution was destined to be a sore trial to him some years later in the Peninsula. There are also a few scathing sentences respecting another officer who was destined to serve, not directly under him, but in co-operation with him in Spain, namely, Lord William Bentinck, who in 1804 succeeded Lord Clive as Governor of Madras. Whig writers have conspired to exalt this painstaking though very mediocre man, but Arthur Wellesley took his measure correctly at once. As to Lake, he naturally and rightly kept his opinions to himself; and yet nothing is more instructive than to compare the methods of Lake and Wellesley. Lake, though sixty years of age, was a fine fighting soldier, of fiery courage and energy, who, moreover, was always loyal to his officers and most careful of his men. He fought brilliant actions and won extraordinary victories, but he also made culpable mistakes, which were more than errors of judgment, and was too fond of rough-and-ready methods. One looks to him in vain for the foresight and sagacity with which Wellesley provided for everything—safety of communications, establishment of advanced bases, organisation of transport and supply—and left nothing to chance.

In March Wellesley paid a brief visit to Bom-

bay, and then returned to Poona to look to the settlement of affairs there. It is noteworthy that
amid the requirements for the subsidiary force of
the Peishwa, he assigned a prominent place to a
regular establishment of transport-bullocks. After
visits to Madras and Calcutta he returned in January 1805 to his work at Seringapatam, where he
suffered from an attack of fever which caused him
to embark in March for England. He was, however, not less sick in heart than in body. Just before starting he heard that he had been created a
Knight of the Bath by the King; but from the East
India Company, despite of his great services, he
had received no reward, nothing, indeed, but in-
jury. There was little prospect of further military
usefulness in India, and he could depart from it
with a good conscience since there was no longer
special duty required of him.

He brought home with him a little fortune of
some thirty or forty thousand pounds, the great
bulk of it prize-money for the campaign of Seringapatam, and every penny of it legitimately gained.
Many a man in his place would have accumulated,
by means which were not then frowned upon, three
or four times that sum, for it must be remembered
that in Mysore he was an absolute autocrat. He

brought back also bodily health much improved, despite of occasional fever, by a hot climate and by constant life in a tent; for during three years he rarely, if ever, slept in a house. He had gathered further vast experience in every branch, down to the minutest detail, of civil and military administration. Lastly, he had acquired the habit, already mentioned, of extreme abstinence in food and drink, and a passion for rice and for a daily bath, which latter at that time was a luxury practically unknown in England. But what he took from India is as nothing as to that which he gave, namely, the tradition of integrity in pecuniary matters, of justice to all men, of protective kindness towards the native population, encouragement to deserving officers, and ruthless hunting of the idle and inefficient. As to the conduct of campaigns he wrought neither more nor less than a revolution. Never before in India had armies been so well supplied, so orderly, so strictly disciplined, and so rapid in their movements. He imparted the secret of his success to many, not always with great profit, for few possessed his quickness of insight and still fewer the amazing energy and industry which prompted him to master every detail. Indeed it may be urged with truth that his traditions were not, in general, of long-endurance. He received many tokens of appreciation from various bodies on quitting India—a sword from the British officers in Calcutta, a gold table-service from the officers who had fought under him, an address from the native inhabitants of Seringapatam, thanking him for the tranquillity that they had enjoyed under his rule. But appreciation is one thing, and imitation is another. Arthur Wellesley after all held but a subordinate station; and something more than seven years of good example was needed to pierce the crust of indolence, incapacity, and corruption which enwrapped the kernel of Indian administration.

So all the old evils remained, and his warnings as to the worst of them were quickly justified. Within fifteen months of his departure there was a dangerous mutiny of Sepoys at Vellore, a rising which, but for the astonishing gallantry and resource of a single officer, Colonel Gillespie, might have shaken British rule to its foundation. In 1809 came the still more sinister mutiny of officers in the Madras Presidency, verifying Wellesley's forebodings as to the peril of such a corporate body. Then, in the matter of campaigns, the Afghan War of 1839–1842 was an extreme of mismanagement, ignorance, and ineptitude. Again, both Ellenborough and Dalhousie took the field with their armies when they had much better have stayed away and minded their own business, as Mornington, thanks to his brother's advice, had done in 1799. On the other hand, Charles Napier in his campaign in Scinde in 1843 proved himself in every respect Arthur Wellesley's good pupil. All, therefore, of his work was not lost; and yet perhaps the greatest testimony to its worth is to be found in a letter from Sir Robert Farquhar, a correspondent in Madras, who writing to Wellesley in February 1810 just after the mutiny of officers had been suppressed, urged that only his arrival as Governor-General and Commander-in-Chief could restore order and save the country. Such was the impression which this colonel of five-and-thirty left upon one of the ablest of his contemporaries in India.

CHAPTER III

WELLESLEY reached England in September 1805 at a most interesting time. Ever since the renewal of the war in May 1803 the terror of a French invasion had hung over England, and the darkness had only just been dispersed. The first gleam of light had come in April when a treaty of alliance had been signed with Russia. Austria joined that alliance on the 9th of August; and on the 22nd Napoleon broke up his camp at Boulogne and marched for the Danube. Pitt seeing, as he hoped, an opportunity for the recovery of Hanover from the French, at the end of October embarked about eleven thousand men for the Weser; and in December this force was reinforced to a strength of twenty-five thousand men under the command of Lord Cathcart; Sir Arthur Wellesley being entrusted with the first brigade of this reinforcement. But meanwhile Napoleon had, on the 20th of October, made an end of the Austrian army of the Danube by the capitulation of Ulm, and on the 2nd of December he defeated both Austrians and Russians at Austerlitz. Austria thereupon

[73]

withdrew from the contest; and Prussia accepted
Hanover as the price of alliance with France.
Therewith the whole mission of Cathcart's force,
which was partly to tempt, partly to force Prussia
to join the coalition, was brought to naught, and
in February 1804 the troops were re-embarked for
England.   This was the last of many like abortive
enterprises undertaken by Pitt who died on the
23rd of January 1806.

On his return Arthur Wellesley was sent with his
brigade to Hastings, where he attended quietly to
its training.   He had much to learn about the
changes that had taken place in the army during
his absence in India.   First and foremost of these
was the success of the Duke of York in the post
which he had taken up in 1796 as Commander-in-
Chief of the Horse Guards.   The Duke had
organised a most efficient staff at headquarters, and
had already done much towards the improvement
of order, system, and discipline.   In brief, the
army was now under military and not civil control.
Further, since the renewal of the war in 1803 the
whole nation had been called under arms, though
with a confusion, mismanagement, and imbecility
that can hardly be credited.   Addington's government, fearful of imposing by compulsion in every

able-bodied citizen his natural duty to defend his country, had permitted the formation of countless bodies of volunteers; and this weakness in allowing men to evade real military service, combined with gross mishandling of the Militia Laws, had gone far to deprive both Militia and Regular Army of their lawful share of recruits. Sundry heroic measures had been passed by Addington and, after his fall, by Pitt to fill the empty ranks of the regulars, but without success. Bounties were still high; recruits were still scarce; and only the crimps flourished. And now in this year 1806 William Windham had come forward with a new scheme. He advocated the voluntary enlistment of soldiers no longer for life, as heretofore, but for a short term, with option of re-engagement for second and third terms, and with a slight increase of pay at the end of each term. By this measure Windham was confident that he could obtain at a cheap rate an endless supply of recruits. Military men, though divided in opinion, were not so sanguine. Sir John Moore, when the project was submitted to him, tossed it contemptuously aside, saying that it was idle to talk of keeping the army up to strength without compulsion. Moore proved to be right, and in due time we shall find Wellington in the

Peninsula much embarrassed by the claims of men, whose period of service had expired, to immediate discharge.

There was another military reform, passed during the Parliamentary session of 1805, which was causing many military men to shake their heads. Until that year regimental courts-martial had been not so much courts of law as family tribunals. The members were not sworn to do justice nor witnesses to tell the truth. The obligations of both were considered as a matter of honour; and the system had worked well for the maintenance of discipline. Officers and men were well content, and desired nothing better. But some busy, foolish person in the House of Commons insisted that witnesses at regimental courts-martial should be placed upon their oath, and that the members of the Court should be sworn to decide according to the weight of evidence. Every officer of standing was against the change, which they thought unnecessary at any time and most impolitic in the midst of a great war. But it is a weakness with politicians, who rarely understand their own business, to aspire to set right the business of all other people; and the reform was duly carried through Parliament. Then it was found that

[76]

soldiers had no more conscience about perjuring themselves than other men, but that officers were considerably more squeamish. A delinquent private brought forward half a dozen comrades, of equal blackguardism with himself, to testify to his innocence of the crime wherewith he was charged; and the officers, feeling themselves bound to decide in agreement with the testimony laid before them, whether true or false, acquitted the accused. The result was that it became practically impossible to convict a prisoner before a regimental court-martial, and that these courts, which had upheld discipline admirably until 1805, failed completely to do so after that year. This was the principal cause of the misbehaviour, of which later Wellington so bitterly complained, of his troops in the Peninsula.

There were, however, other details which could be discussed with greater satisfaction. Despite of all mistakes, the nation had in general showed a fine spirit under the menace of invasion; and a false alarm had brought every description of troops, from regulars to volunteers, eagerly and enthusiastically to the rendezvous. The arrangements of the headquarter staff likewise had shown wisdom and forethought; and a whole scheme for taking up transport, whether for ordinary purposes or to convey bodies of troops swiftly from point to point, had been arranged in every district. The training had improved, and Sir John Moore by a special course of instruction had brought his brigade at Shorncliffe to the highest degree of efficiency and discipline.

Moreover, there was a new invention brought forward by Major Henry Shrapnel of the Artillery at the Royal Arsenal, spherical case shot. Of course everyone knew all about grapeshot—a bag of bullets fired from a cannon and very effective up to a range of two hundred yards—but Shrapnel's projectile, something quite new, a spherical iron shell filled with bullets which was thrown from a howitzer with a time-fuse, and produced the effect of long-range grape. What the extreme range might be was doubtful, but the spherical case was certainly effective up to eight hundred yards, and some said up to a thousand or even twelve hundred yards. It had been used for the first time in service at the capture of Surinam in 1804, and the gunners thought there was a great future for it.

Such, we may guess, was some of the military gossip which came to Arthur Wellesley's ears at Hastings in 1806; but meanwhile he was occupied with homelier matters. Finding that his old love, Lady Katherine Pakenham, still cared for him and was still single, he married her in April; and it may be said at once that she bore him two children, in 1807 and 1808, but was not the right wife for him. In June he entered the House of Commons as member for Rye, breaking his resolution to have nothing more to do with politics in order to defend his brother Mornington, now raised to the rank of Marquess Wellesley, against attacks upon his administration in India. What time may have been left free to him from these distractions to attend to the training of his brigade, we know not; but it is certain that later in the Peninsula he declared one of his three regiments, the Thirty-sixth, famous in the German War as the Worcesters, to be the best in his army.

Events in Europe were now moving apace, though so far England had contributed little to the war except Nelson's victory at Trafalgar in October 1805. But a little detachment of six thousand men, under Sir James Craig, had been sent with a kind of roving commission to the Mediterranean, and this seemed to be a likely field for British operations. One of the conditions that Napoleon exacted when he granted peace to Austria in December 1805 was that she should acknowledge him as King of Italy. Not the least of his ambitions was to make the Mediterranean a French lake, and, since the British held Malta, it was of the first importance to him to hold Sicily. No sooner, therefore, was his treaty with Austria signed than he ordered one of his armies to march into the Kingdom of Naples, declared that the house of Bourbon had ceased to reign there, and raised his brother Joseph to their throne in their stead. The Neapolitans made no effort to resist the invasion. The French took possession of Naples itself, and were on the point of occupying Sicily, when Craig, who had seen what was coming, forestalled them by throwing his troops into Messina.

Herein Craig, who acted against the advice of the British diplomatists on the spot, rendered his country a very signal service. In 1799 Sir Charles Stuart, a very great soldier whose career was too soon cut short by death, had likewise landed at Messina, rallied the Sicilians to him, made all provision for the defence of the island, and pointed out its transcendent value as a base from which to operate against the French in Italy. Very fertile, rich in supplies and abounding in good harbours, it would have been perfect for the purpose; and

Italy, a long narrow peninsula, would have made an ideal field for what are called amphibious operations. In fact, if our Ministers had known their business the Peninsular War would have been fought in Italy and not in Spain, and would have begun in 1806 and not in 1808. Possibly Craig, if he had remained in command, would have initiated operations which would have compelled Ministers to reinforce him and have led them in the right way. But Craig's health failed; and his successor, Sir John Stuart, was an impostor, while the naval commander on the spot, Sidney Smith, was a shallow mountebank. This pair, each thinking chiefly how he might gain all credit for himself, made a raid into Calabria, where Stuart, or rather his army for him, fought and won a brilliant little action on the 4th of July at Maida. The numbers on each side were nearly equal, the British counting about six thousand and the French rather more. The two forces met on a plain as smooth as a billiard-table; both were drawn up in line; and the British by sheer superiority of musketry blasted the French off the field with very heavy loss. This result must have set all military men thinking, and beyond a doubt Arthur Wellesley among them; but Stuart and Sidney Smith made no effort to

glance further at the situation in England and in
Europe.

Despite of the reverse suffered by Napoleon at
Eylau, the outlook for England was not reassur-
ing. Windham's scheme, based upon short service
for the regulars and national training for home
defences, had completely broken down. He had
swept away the Volunteers, but had created no new
force to take their place; and the result was that
few regular troops could be spared from internal
defence to take the offensive beyond sea. The late
Ministry had involved itself in petty operations in
Egypt, with some vague idea of counteracting
French influence there, and the enterprise had
ended disastrously. More regiments had been sent
to South America; and no one could say when they
would return. Castlereagh reckoned that at the
very most he could not spare more than twelve
thousand men; and hardly had he begun even to
count upon this small handful when the news
of the Sepoy revolt at Vellore caused him to
send four thousand of them immediately to India.
Then there was a question whether a force should
not be landed in Pomerania to help the Russians;
and the King's German Legion, seven thousand
strong, under Lord Cathcart, was actually disem-

barked at Stralsund early in July, with the promise of more troops to follow. But meanwhile Napoleon had recovered himself, beaten the Russians decisively at Friedland on the 14th of June, and taken the Tsar to his arms by the Treaty of Tilsit on the 25th. With Russia for his ally he designed to close every port in Europe to British ships, and bring England to her knees by putting an end to her commerce and so cutting at the root of her financial resources.

This was the worst moment of the Great War since the mutiny at Spithead in 1797, or at any rate it seemed to be so. In actual fact it was the beginning of the end for Napoleon, for the campaign in Poland had been terrifically costly in men, and from 1806 onward he was compelled to make heavy overdrafts, so to speak, upon his account of conscripts. Castlereagh had the courage to meet the crisis firmly. He drafted twenty-eight thousand of the Militia into the Regular Army, and by measures of unprecedented severity used the ballot to raise forty-four thousand fresh militiamen to fill the gaps. He also took up tonnage enough for the eight or ten thousand men, which alone were at his disposal for the moment, to enable him to transport them to any point at the shortest notice.

was a double danger. If Napoleon gained possession of the Danish fleet, not only might he in his own good time use it, with the Danish ports for base, for invasion of England, but he might immediately cut off the retreat of the King's German Legion from Stralsund, which place was already invested by the French on the side of the land. It was resolved, therefore, to send a powerful fleet to the Baltic at once, to be joined as soon as possible by twenty thousand troops from England and the seven thousand men of the German Legion from Stralsund. A diplomatic agent was sent forward to arrange, amicably if possible, that the British should take possession of the Danish fleet, pledging themselves to restore it upon the conclusion of a general peace; but no one dreamed that such a demand would be complied with.

The preparations were made with extreme secrecy; and on the 29th of July, ten days after the issue of the orders, the transports sailed, the whole being under the command of Lord Cathcart, with Sir Harry Burrard for his second, Sir David Baird for one of his divisional generals, and Arthur Wellesley for one of his brigadiers. Wellesley was in charge of what was called the Reserve—four and a half choice battalions, including three which

had been trained by Sir John Moore at Shorncliffe
and were later to be the nucleus of the famous
Light Division. There is no need to follow the
operations in detail. The force was landed on the
16th of August in the Sound, about ten miles north
of Copenhagen, Wellesley's Reserve going first
ashore to cover the disembarkation of the rest.
The investment of Copenhagen was completed on
the 18th, and the army settled down to the work of
the seige. On the 26th a relieving force of Danes
made its appearance to south of the town, and
Wellesley was detached with the Reserve, two light
batteries and a small body of all three arms of the
King's German Legion, to deal with it. A manœuvre to attack the enemy in front and cut off their
retreat in rear was frustrated by their unexpected
retirement; and Wellesley then followed them up
to their next position, intending once again to assail
their front himself, while a part of his force, fetch-
ing a wide compass, should fall upon their flank.
Since this flanking column did not make its appearance at the appointed hour, Wellesley attacked
by himself. The Danes, for the most part half-
disciplined levies, made a poor resistance and were
easily dispersed with the loss of many men killed
and wounded, and fifteen hundred prisoners.

There is nothing more to be said of the campaign except that Wellesley, as always, behaved to the people of the country with gentleness and consideration, and took care that they should not be molested by his troops. On the 5th of September the Danish General asked for an armistice, and Wellesley was chosen as one of the Commissioners to draw up the capitulation, which was signed on the 7th. A week later he obtained leave of absence to return to his duties in Ireland, and by the end of September was again in London.

This blow came as a stunning surprise to Napoleon, yet hardly had the Danish fleet been secured, before the British Government realised that he meant to indemnify himself by seizing instead the Portuguese fleet at Lisbon. At the end of July the Emperor assembled an army under Junot at Bayonne, gained the consent of Spain to its passage through Spanish territory by promising to give Portugal to her, and on the 20th of October declared war upon Portugal and ordered Junot to cross the frontier. The British Ministers, anticipating some such stroke, had instructed Cathcart to send back ten thousand men as early as possible from Copenhagen, and Napoleon, probably having information of this, directed Junot to hasten his march upon Lisbon. With great difficulty the British ambassador prevailed upon the Prince Regent of Portugal to sail to Brazil, and to turn what had been a Portuguese colony into the home of the royal family; and Junot entered Lisbon just in time to see the sails of the Portuguese fleet in the offing, having missed his prize by a few hours only. So unmercifully had he hurried his wretched men forward over a rugged and miserable country, having, according to the French rule, made no provision for their subsistence, that he entered the Portuguese capital with barely one-tenth of his troops at his back, and these were no more than a mob of undisciplined stragglers, with little clothing, no shoes, no ammunition, and with arms ruined by ill-usage.

We shall have to do with this army of Junot's before very long; but meanwhile the British Government, seeing that Napoleon was excluding England from all the markets of Europe, had begun seriously to contemplate abandoning them and seeking new markets in the new world. They built great hopes upon the departure of the Portuguese royal family to Brazil for one thing, and, under the inspiration of two or three unscrupulous adventurers, they entertained vague ideas of ap-

propriating sundry Spanish colonies in Central
and South America, notably Mexico and Vene-
zuela. The fate of the expedition to Buenos Aires,
which had returned in defeat and disgrace to the
British Isles in October 1807, seemed not to deter
them; and Arthur Wellesley, to whom they turned
for advice, drew up for them many memoranda
and plans of campaign. In one of these, written
before the British troops had left for Rio de la
Plata, is a scheme for an attack on Mexico which
must, I think, have been imposed upon him by the
wild brain of William Windham. The principal
force of about twelve thousand men was to be based
on Jamaica; three thousand men from Buenos
Aires were to join them there; and, finally, three
thousand Sepoys were to sail from Calcutta by
way of Penang and Botany Bay, and thence westward across the whole length of the Southern
Ocean to Cape Horn and round it up to the west
coast of Mexico, a voyage which, Wellesley esti-
mated, would last five months. Such voyages
were not unknown in those days. Some of the
transports returning from Buenos Aires took one
hundred and eighty days to reach England. But
to convoy a fleet from Sydney to the Cape of Good
Hope, with no possibility of calling at any port on

the way, was a responsibility which no naval officer would readily have taken. In fact these papers of Wellesley's must not all of them be taken too seriously. If Ministers had given less attention to these distant enterprises and more to the Mediterranean, they could have shortened Napoleon's domination of Europe and regained European markets with far less effort and searching of heart.

Fate, however, was kind enough to give them a second chance. In October 1807 Napoleon, in order to compel the closing of all European ports to the British, began to concentrate large forces upon the Spanish frontier; and in February 1808, upon a very flimsy pretext, he ordered from seventy to eighty thousand men to pass it. The principal fortresses were mastered by treachery; Madrid was occupied by the French on the 23rd of March; and in July it was announced that the Bourbons had ceased to rule in Spain and that Joseph Bonaparte reigned in their stead. Long before that time the whole of the country had risen in arms to drive the French out, Madrid setting the example by a savage insurrection on the 2nd of May. The province of Asturias gave the lead by declaring, with magnificent audacity, formal war upon Napoleon on the 24th of May, and despatching emissaries to seek help from England; and with amazing rapidity the rest of the northern provinces and those of the east and south organised local governments and began to raise troops. Sir Hew Dalrymple, the Governor of Gibraltar, ever since his arrival at the Rock in November 1806 had juditaciously cultivated the friendship of General Castaños, the Spanish Commandant in Andalusia; and, after the French invasion of Spain, Castaños eagerly appealed to him for help. As it happened, Dalrymple had a few troops at his disposal. The ten thousand men demanded from Lord Cathcart after the surrender of Copenhagen had been duly despatched home; and in December eight thousand of them, under General Brent Spencer, one of Cathcart's brigadiers, had been ordered to embark for the Mediterranean. After much delay, owing to stormy weather, Spencer reached Gibraltar early in March, sent half of his force—all troops of the German Legion—to Sicily, and remained with five thousand British infantry at the Rock to await instructions.

Meanwhile the Spanish insurrection progressed with astonishing success. Napoleon directed his main efforts southward against Andalusia, Murcia, and Valencia, confining his efforts in the north to the securing of Santander and Zaragoza. But the column which attempted to seize Valencia was repulsed; and that which marched into Andalusia was actually surrounded and compelled to surrender at Baylen. Zaragoza defended itself desperately. Only in Leon, where the Spanish armies had imprudently taken the offensive, could the Emperor boast of any victory. Moreover, in June, Portugal also had risen in revolt, compelling Junot to withdraw nearly all of his outlying troops and to concentrate the bulk of his army at Lisbon. Through all this time Spencer, having no orders, sailed backwards and forwards along the coast between Gibraltar and Lisbon, rarely landing a man, but giving everywhere countenance and encouragement. Thereby he added materially to the difficulties and embarrassments of the French generals, who, however ready to take risks against ill-armed and undisciplined Spanish levies, naturally recoiled from the prospect of finding one of their flying columns confronted by even five thousand perfectly trained troops. Never was there a more excellent example of the advantage conferred by command of the sea. At last, after two months of this wandering, Spencer, on the 15th of July, received instructions from home that an expedition under Sir Arthur Wellesley was about to sail from Cork and that he must await Sir Arthur's orders at Cadiz. The die was cast; and the hand that had thrown it was Arthur Wellesley's own.

The news of the Spanish insurrection reached England in May, and at once Wellesley sat down and wrote a memorandum recommending that the entire force at disposal of Ministers should be sent to join Spencer's detachment off the coast of Spain, in readiness to take advantage of any opening. In the first week of June the Commander-in-Chief was directed to raise the numbers of the infantry to eight thousand men, exclusive of cavalry and artillery; and on the 14th of June Wellesley received his letter of service to take command of the whole expedition. Its numerical weakness was due to the fact that Ministers had sent eleven thousand men under Sir John Moore upon a fool's errand to Sweden, with some vague idea of protecting the mad king of that country, who was the last of their continental allies, against the invasion of an overwhelming force of French, Danes, and Russians. However, weak or strong, Wellesley began to prepare his army for work at once looking, as usual, into every detail himself. The first difficulty was that the artillery had no horses, for their original destination had been South America, which was so remote that horses in any number could not be transported thither. This was overcome by taking the teams of the Irish Waggon Train, a small establishment of two troops which was maintained for the transport and supply of mobile columns in Ireland. But Wellesley was not inclined to land in a strange country without some regular organisation, however small, for transport and supply; so he demanded not only the horses but the officers and the drivers; and after a struggle he obtained them. More he could not do, for, since it was still uncertain where the force would act and how long it might be kept on board ship before landing, it was idle to think of filling ships with the four thousand animals which, at the very least, would have been needed to make the force mobile. Indeed the Government had not horse-transports enough to carry half that number, to say nothing of their forage and water. In actual fact the number of horses of every description that were embarked fell below six hundred, and the number of wheeled vehicles, including the gun-carriages, the ammunition waggons and their forge-carts, counted just forty-three, of which four only were transport-waggons. The animals, together with a thousand dragoons and artillerymen, filled twenty-one vessels, with an aggregate burden of six thousand tons. Modern soldiers, who have seen men shipped off for long distances over sea, with their organisation and equipment perfect in every respect, have little idea of the work thrown upon a commander-in-chief who not only had no Army Service Corps and no ambulances, but whose cavalry and infantry were subject to one department, his artillery and engineers to a second, and his commissariat and transport to a third. The only thing that can be said is that things were at least better in England than in India.

After some delay through foul winds the armament sailed from Cork on the 13th of July, Wellesley himself starting a day earlier in a frigate for Coruña. On the 15th Ministers decided to send a further reinforcement of five thousand men at once, and that eleven thousand more, which were returning from Sweden under Sir John Moore, should follow as soon as possible. The entire force, thus increased to thirty thousand men, was to be placed under the supreme command of Sir Hew Dalrymple, with Sir Harry Burrard for second, an arrangement which seems to have been con-

trived for the express purpose of keeping Moore
in a subordinate position. Sir John was incom-
parably abler than either Burrard or Dalrymple,
but he was in bad odour with Ministers because
he had given them bluntly to understand that it
had been folly to send his troops to Sweden, and
that he intended to bring them back. As all
three of these officers were senior to Wellesley, his
prospects of long tenure of independent command
were not bright; but, until they arrived, he was
authorised to proceed with operations in Portugal.

Arriving at Coruña on the 20th Wellesley consulted the provisional government, or Junta, of
Galicia, but, obtaining from them no satisfactory
information, went on to Oporto. Here he met the
Supreme Junta of all Portugal, which again could
give none but the vaguest intelligence; but on the
other hand, there was a letter from the Admiral,
Sir Charles Cotton, to say that the fort of Figueira
in Mondego Bay had been placed in his hands by
the Portuguese insurgents and was occupied by
four hundred British Marines. This was satisfactory, for Mondego Bay is a hundred and fifty
miles nearer to Lisbon than Vigo, which had
seemed to be the nearest port open to him. He
obtained orders for one hundred and fifty horses

and five hundred mules to be ready for him on disembarkation, directed the troops to prepare for a landing in Mondego Bay, and sailed on to the Tagus. Here he found valuable intelligence awaiting him from Spencer as to the strength of the French in Portugal, and, after consultation with the Admiral, decided definitely to disembark on the Mondego. By the 30th of July he was again with his army, where he received the despatches that announced the coming of reinforcements and the early prospect of his supersession. He answered that, whatever happened, he would do his best, and would not hurry operations unduly in order to secure the credit of their success.

On the 1st of August the disembarkation began —a tedious and dangerous business, for the anchorage, though protected from the north,[1] lay open to the west, and the surf on the Portuguese coast is heavy. The troops therefore were perforce landed in boats, not without accidents and loss of men drowned; and it was five days before the nine thousand men with their horses, artillery, and stores were all ashore. On the 6th Spencer

[1] The coast is subject to sudden and fierce northerly gales: the writer knows the *nordano* (as this wind is called) by experience, and can understand why Wellesley above all sought shelter from it.

arrived with his detachment, having with sound
instinct made straight for the Tagus upon learning that the Spaniards no longer needed him in
Andalusia. Three more days were occupied in
disembarking his troops, making eight days in all
for the landing of fifteen thousand men; but
Wellesley had not wasted his time. He had begun
by drawing up with his own hand a table for his
commissaries as to the organisation of the transport, giving even details for the loads of pack-
mules and ox-waggons; and he had actually
obtained carriage enough for thirteen days' supplies and for his reserve of ammunition, besides
horses enough to strengthen his own gun-teams
and to mount sixty of his two hundred dragoons.
But this effort exhausted the resources of the
country round the Mondego, and still left Spencer's artillery without a single horse. Next he
organised his army into six brigades, distributing
among them his eighteen field-pieces; and thus
after ten strenuous days ashore he was able to
begin work in earnest.

Meanwhile, his information as to Junot's strength
was not very exact. Spencer had given it as twenty
thousand; Wellesley reckoned it at eighteen thousand; and, since he knew that Junot still kept

garrisons in the fortresses of Almeida and Elvas on the Spanish frontier, he put down the force actually at disposal for defence of Lisbon at fourteen thousand only. He knew further, that a column of seven thousand men under General Loison had recently been detached in the direction of Elvas, and he therefore concluded that Junot would be powerless at Lisbon until Loison's return. As a matter of fact Junot had twenty-six thousand troops in all; and had Wellesley been aware of this he might have hesitated to disembark, much more to march on Lisbon. As things were, he broke up his camp on the Mondego on the 10th of August and started along the road by the coast for the capital with about fourteen thousand men, his supply-ships moving parallel with him by sea. On the 11th he picked up some fourteen hundred Portuguese infantry and three hundred cavalry, and on the 15th reached Caldas, where he halted for a day to replenish his supplies. He had already intelligence that Junot had pushed forward some five or six thousand men under General Delaborde to observe his movements and to cover the return of Loison to Lisbon; and on the 15th his advanced parties engaged Delaborde's outposts at Obidos. He knew also on the night of the 15th that Loison had passed through Rio Mayor, about ten miles to east of him, pointing south; but as there was a road leading from Rio Mayor directly to Obidos, he had to guard against the possibility that Loison might take it and come in upon his flank. On the morning of the 17th he advanced to the attack.

Obidos stands on a rocky hill in the midst of a plain which is almost encircled by a great horse-shoe of very steep and rugged mountains. Through this plain the road to Lisbon ran due south, skirting the village of Roliça, at the foot of a broad, low hill about two miles from Obidos, and climbing the horseshoe close to its tip about half a mile farther on. Delaborde, who had little more than four thousand infantry with one weak regi-ment of cavalry and five guns, had occupied the hill of Roliça, and Wellesley, who even after detaching his Portuguese to watch for Loison, had fourteen thousand men and eighteen guns, man-œuvred his opponent out of his position with little difficulty, and forced him to retire to the summit of the horseshoe. He then gave his orders for shift-ing Delaborde from this position also by turning both flanks, and when this was done, by assailing his centre. But four British battalions in the centre by some mistake attacked prematurely. The hills were so steep and rough that the men could hardly ascend them without using their hands, and only after four repulses did they succeed in establishing themselves on the summit. Delaborde who had fought his action with extreme skill, never retiring until the latest possible moment, then retreated, still handling his troops admirably. But he had waited just a little too long; and, as the British pressed on, his men became unsteady about a mile in rear of the summit, and abandoned a few prisoners and three guns. Wellesley, however, pursued him no farther, being still uncertain about Loison, while the ground on the line of Delaborde's retreat was perfectly designed by nature for endless rearguard actions. So the action ended with credit to both parties, for, though the French had only five battalions on the field, four and a half British battalions alone had engaged them and driven them back; and the casualties of the French numbered six hundred against the British five hundred. To the end of his days Wellington spoke with admiration of the stubborn spirit shown by the French at Roliça.

On the 18th Wellesley heard that the first batch of reinforcements was off the coast, and, having

decided that they should land at the mouth of the
river Maceira, struck south-westward and took up
a position on the 19th at Vimeiro to cover the disembarkation. By the evening of the 20th most of
the five thousand men had been landed; and Wellesley issued his orders to renew the march on the
morrow. But now Sir Harry Burrard appeared in
a frigate; and Wellesley, on going aboard to see
him, received his commands not to move. Burrard's reasons were by no means unsound—a man
can always find good arguments for inaction,—
but they were a great disappointment to Wellesley,
who was quite prepared to advance at all risks.
He cancelled his orders, therefore, and remained
stationary. His chosen position was a steep ridge,
from four to five hundred feet high and about
four miles long, extending eastward from the sea in-
land. This feature is cut into two equal parts by
the steep, rocky gorge of the river Maceira, which
parts I shall call the western and eastern ridge.
At the mouth of the gorge on the southern side—
that is the side from which the enemy was to be
expected—lies a low round hill, and on its northern
slopes stands the village of Vimeiro. Wellesley
who had not occupied this position with an immediate view to defence, had for convenience of water

placed most of his troops on the western ridge, excepting two brigades which were stationed on Vimeiro Hill. His cavalry, artillery, and transport were all parked on a flat ground behind that hill, ready to march off on the morrow. Since Vimeiro Hill constituted a strong advanced post, or bastion, to the main ridge, it is evident that Wellesley had not taken up his ground with the idea of awaiting an attack, otherwise he would have placed his transport farther in rear.

Before 1 a.m. of the 21st, however, an officer of the German Legion galloped up to headquarters with the news that the French were advancing, twenty thousand strong, and were within an hour's march. Wellesley was incredulous, but ordered six additional guns to be moved to Vimeiro Hill; and it was not till 7 a.m., when the army had long been under arms, that the first sign of an enemy was seen. Junot had concentrated the bulk of his troops, but had told off so many of them for the defence of Lisbon that he had advanced to meet Wellesley with no more than thirteen thousand men and twenty-three guns. After reconnaissance of the position he decided to attack the eastern ridge; and accordingly he directed two of his four brigades with seven guns to fall upon Vimeiro Hill

from the south and east, and a third, under General
Brennier, to fetch a wide compass, and simultaneously to attack the main ridge from the east.
Wellesley, watching their movements, divined their
intentions and had plenty of time to shift from the
western to the eastern ridge sufficient troops to
bring Junot's plan to nought. On Junot's side
the fight was grossly mismanaged. The two brigades launched against Vimeiro Hill came into
action more or less together, but were badly beaten,
the more easily that they attacked in dense columns
which exposed them both in front and flanks to the
fire of the British line. Brennier's column lost its
way; and Solignac's brigade, which Junot sent
some time later to support Brennier, attacked by
itself and was utterly defeated. Junot's last reserve of four battalions, which he very rashly threw
also into the fight too early, shared the same fate;
and, when Brennier at length found his true point
of attack he, in his turn, was driven back with
heavy loss. By noon the battle was over. Every
regiment of French infantry had been heavily
punished, and fourteen out of twenty-four guns
had been taken. Moreover, the infantry in its
confusion had fled eastward instead of southward,
leaving open the line of their retreat. Solignac's

brigade, indeed, had entangled itself hopelessly in a ravine and was only waiting to be surrounded. On the other hand, only twelve British battalions had been engaged, and they had not suffered heavily and were flushed with victory, while seven battalions had not fired a shot. Wellesley was eager to follow up his success, which would practically have assured him the capture of Junot's army; but Sir Harry Burrard, who had come ashore, forbade pursuit. He had left Wellesley alone to fight the battle; but now he interposed. The transport of the army, from the first insufficient, was now diminished by the flight of many drivers with their carts and the assignment of many other vehicles to the carriage of the wounded. Wellington was rightly prepared to risk all difficulties and privations to make his victory complete; but Burrard was too cautious and timid to give him a free hand. Junot therefore was allowed to escape. His casualties amounted to eighteen hundred, whereas those of the British did not exceed seven hundred and twenty.

Burrard had hardly assumed control before he was superseded, on the 22nd, by the arrival of Sir Hew Dalrymple from Gibraltar. Dalrymple had never commanded in the field, had seen no active service since 1794, and for some years had performed administrative duties only. As an administrator he showed capacity and sound judgment; but with an army in the field he was nervous and ill at ease; and when Wellesley laid before him his plans for cutting off Junot's army from Lisbon—for it was not yet too late—he rejected them and declined to move at all until the morrow. A few hours later Junot sent in a flag of truce for the evacuation of Portugal by the French under a convention. Wellesley, being consulted, advised acceptance of the offer and himself signed the preliminary agreement. As usual he faced facts. The great opportunity for capturing every French soldier in Portugal had passed away; and it was everything now to secure Lisbon without bloodshed. Eventually it was agreed by the Convention of Cintra that the French troops should be embarked with arms, baggage, artillery, and private property to some port on the Atlantic coast of France; and on the 9th of September the entry of the British into Lisbon brought Wellesley's first Peninsular campaign to an end.

Meanwhile Moore's division had also arrived, raising the force to a total of some thirty thousand men, which Dalrymple was utterly incompetent to

command. Everyone came for orders to Wellesley; three officers senior to him, who had arrived
with Moore, waived their rank that he might command his division; and Moore himself urged Dalrymple that, in the event of further operations, any
force that might be detached should be placed under
Wellesley. But Dalrymple did not like Wellesley, and the officers who had served under him
testified their dislike for Dalrymple by sending
Wellesley a piece of plate. Sir Arthur himself
felt quite as much discontent as any man in his
army; and he went the length of approaching
Moore to say that the present state of things
could not go on, that there must be a new
Commander-in-Chief, and that the army looked to
Moore himself to take up the post. This was flat
mutiny; but Moore was not without experience of
such things. After the death of Abercromby in
Egypt, Sir John had been urged by the rest of the
generals present to oust General Hutchinson from
the supreme command and assume it himself. He
had then answered by recalling those who thus
tempted him to a sense of their duty; and he now
informed Wellesley, kindly but with firmness, that
he would enter into no intrigue against the
Commander-in-Chief appointed by the King's

Ministers. The two men warmed towards each other in this their first intimate meeting. It was destined to be the last, for on the 18th of September Wellesley went home on leave to England, which Moore was never to see again.

The news of the Convention of Cintra had arrived before him, and Ministers were as frantic with vexation as the nation at large was indignant. Wellesley, as the man who had signed the armistice, was held up to particular reprobation. A Court of Enquiry was appointed to report upon the whole matter, with the result that it declared no officer to be in fault, and expressed the very reasonable opinion that, if the chief command of an army changed twice in twenty-four hours, it was not surprising if that army remained halted for forty-eight hours. Ministers, who were themselves chiefly to blame for all that had gone wrong, decided to make a scapegoat of Dalrymple and removed him from Gibraltar, where he had done admirable work, in disgrace. Wellesley for his part returned to his work in Ireland, and, when the spring of 1809 came, took his seat as usual in the House of Commons. We have a glimpse of him there at the Committee of Enquiry into the charges of the notorious Mrs. Clark against the Duke of

York, when that clever and shameless adventuress had the impudence actually to quote Sir Arthur Wellesley's name in connection with her nefarious traffic in military commissions. The House received it with a roar of laughter which bore flattering testimony to the high character which he bore, not less in civil than in military circles. He attended the enquiry to the end, and predicted the inevitable resignation of the Duke of York, which was sent in on the 17th of March. Then at the end of March he hurriedly cleared up his Irish business and took leave of the Lord-Lieutenant. He had once again been appointed to the command in Portugal; and, little though he foresaw it, was to return from that country no longer as Sir Arthur Wellesley, member for Rye, but as a peer of the Upper House and Duke of Wellington.

CHAPTER IV

MUCH had happened between Wellesley's departure from Portugal and his orders to return thither. The French army in Spain had been driven by the insurgents behind the Ebro; and a line of undisciplined mobs, called Spanish armies, under incompetent and jealous leaders, called generals, had ranged themselves opposite to them from Tudela north-westward to Reinosa, talking big of driving the invaders out of the country. They left a space in their array to be filled by a British army; for the British Government, augmenting its force in the Peninsula to forty thousand men, had ordered it to co-operate with the Spanish generals. Having originally called in Burrard to exclude Moore from supreme command, the British Ministers, had decided, quite rightly though quite illogically, to place Moore in charge of the field-army and set aside Burrard. Sir Harry, a good soldier, a great gentleman, and an enthusiastic admirer of Moore, had accepted the position loyally, remaining behind at Lisbon without prospect of rank or distinction, and making over to

[113]

Sir John all the best that he had to give. So Moore marched away to the north-east, not forgetting to write home his appreciation of Burrard's generosity, and taking with him, as the only return that he could make, Burrard's son as one of his aides-de-camp.

But, meanwhile, Napoleon by incredible exertion had gathered together two hundred thousand men; and, leading them in person into Spain at the beginning of November, scattered the Spanish armies in all directions. On the 2nd of December he entered Madrid; and Moore discovered that the Spanish hosts, with which he was instructed to co-operate, did not exist. Still there was one thing, a very bold and very dangerous thing, which he could still do; and so it was that on the 19th of December Napoleon learned that Moore, whom he had imagined to be in Portugal, or at any rate in retreat thither, was advancing to north-west of him straight upon the line of his communications with France. Incensed by the English general's temerity he instantly started in pursuit of him with forty thousand men under his personal command, ordering two more corps, each of about the same strength, to hold the British in front and flank. But Moore, prepared, as he said, at any moment to "run for it," had already turned back to his ships at Coruña and was not to be caught. On the 16th of January he fought a battle to cover his embarkation, and in another week his army, excepting some six thousand stragglers who gradually drifted back to Lisbon, was safe in England, ready for further service. Moore, as is well known, fell in the action, and young Harry Burrard likewise was mortally wounded. Harry Burrard the elder went home, and was succeeded in command of the troops left in Portugal by Sir John Cradock, a good soldier but not of the calibre to conduct a campaign which might mean life or death to England. There had been only three British generals great enough for that task: Charles Stuart, who had died in 1807; John Moore, who lay wrapped in his cloak in one of the bastions of Coruña; and the one survivor, Arthur Wellesley, who was discredited in the popular mind by his acceptance of the Convention of Cintra.

There was anxious discussion in the Cabinet as to the measures for prosecuting the war. Austria had approached England in the autumn, secretly declaring her intention of taking up arms in the spring while Napoleon was still entangled with his embarrassments in Spain. This was one reason why these embarrassments should be increased; and the Cabinet decided to make a fresh venture in the Peninsula, starting this time in Spain, from Cadiz, and not from Portugal. The return of Moore's army had caused consternation at home, where for long the great service which he had done was unrecognized. Moreover, Moore had quite correctly declared the Portuguese army to be valueless, and the Portuguese frontier to be indefensible against a superior force; and he had added that, if the French succeeded in Spain, they could not be resisted in Portugal. Good sense, therefore, seemed to point to Spain as the base for future operations; but owing to diplomatic mismanagement the Spanish project came to naught. The Cabinet then conceived the new idea of reorganising the Portuguese army under British officers, paying it and making it almost into a body of British mercenaries. This done, they approached Arthur Wellesley, who delivered his opinion that, given seventy thousand Portuguese soldiers and militia, and twenty thousand British, the French could not conquer Portugal with fewer than one hundred thousand men, and that, if the Spaniards continued to offer resistance, it was extremely improbable that the French could afford so many. Here was

[116]

a definite opinion, worth weighing in view of Austria's coming declaration of war; and, after painful debate, Ministers came to the momentous decision to increase the British force in Portugal to twenty-six thousand men, and to select Arthur Wellesley for the chief command. Castlereagh had a desperate struggle with his colleagues over this appointment, but he prevailed. At the end of March Wellesley accepted the charge, and on the 15th of April 1809 he sailed from Portsmouth for the Tagus.

It is worth while at this point to glance at the condition of the British Army at large. The infantry of the Line consisted of one hundred regiments, nearly every one of which had two battalions, the design being that the second battalion should remain at home and feed the first battalion on foreign service. It was not tacitly understood that the Regular Militia existed chiefly for the purpose of securing and training recruits for the Regular Army; home defence being entrusted to a Local Militia, called into existence by Castlereagh, which was raised by compulsory personal service through the ballot. The system was by no means perfect, but served tolerably well to keep the ranks filled. In addition to the British troops proper, there was the old regular Hanoverian army, now known as the King's German Legion, some twelve thousand excellent troops of all arms; and there were several battalions of foreigners, chiefly attached to the Sixtieth (the old Royal Americans) for service in the West Indies. The full strength of the Regular Army was about thirty thousand cavalry, one hundred and ninety thousand infantry, and seventeen thousand artillery.

In the matter of quality the excellent administration of the Duke of York, who was welcomed back to the command-in-chief in 1811, bore fruit in steady improvement of drill and discipline; though the ill-judged reform of regimental courts-martial had already shown evil results. The infantry were probably the best in the world, and its fire was certainly the most deadly. The cavalry were well mounted and well drilled, but as horse-masters not to be compared to the horse of the German Legion. They knew little either of reconnaissance or vedette-duty; and though they manœuvred beautifully, they were apt to attack at excessive speed and to pass out of control. The artillery was very good, Lord Chatham having shown great ability in the administration of the Ordnance Office; but there were no field-pieces of greater calibre than nine-pounders, which were overmatched by the French twelve-pounders—Napoleon's "pretty girls," as he called them. On the other hand, the British had the advantage in their sole possession of the "long-range grape," which has already been described as the invention of Major Shrapnel. Shell of any kind in those days was fired only from howitzers or mortars, and the proportion of howitzers to field-pieces in a battery was only one to five; but it was common to separate the howitzers from the field-guns and mass them together. Field-pieces fired only grape- and round-shot, the effective range of the latter being from four to five hundred yards. The highest trial of troops in those days was to endure the fire of ricochet round-shot, when they could see the ball bounding over the ground straight towards them, and might not get out of the way. No cavalry in the world, and only British infantry, could long stand firm under ricochet round-shot. The Engineers were a corps of officers only, and included many men of capacity; but their business was supposed to be confined to sieges alone, and such other work as the making of bridges was entrusted to a body called the Staff Corps, founded by the Duke of York in 1799 as, so to speak, the

Commander-in-Chief's engineers, in distinction from the Royal Engineers under the Master-General of the Ordnance. This Staff Corps was the darling of the Quartermaster-General's Department, and, though it numbered only about six hundred of all ranks, was scattered in small bodies all over the Empire. The officers with Wellesley were some of them of very remarkable ability, good surveyors and endowed with singular resource in solving difficult problems of civil engineering.

As to Wellesley's own staff, he was at first his own chief staff-officer, until he gradually trained his subordinates to be efficient. The head of them was the Quartermaster-General, contrary to the practice in India, where the chief of staff then and for fifty years later was the Adjutant-General. Wellesley's Adjutant-General was a compiler of daily returns and no more. The Military Secretary was literally a secretary, who kept a register of the correspondence and wrote what he was told to write. It is significant that it is rare to find the hour of the receipt, and still rarer to see the hour of the despatch noted upon any document. Watches were evidently carried by few officers in those days.

On the whole Wellesley had promising material

under his hand; and the reader may ask why, since
Moore had commanded forty thousand men, no
34-Wellington DOO 12S 22-15 Sept. 10 No. 16
more than twenty-six thousand should have been
allowed to Wellesley.   The answer is that the Government had determined to make their main diversion in Austria's favour in another quarter.   No
English statesman can be easy when Antwerp is
in an enemy's hands; and the design was to strike
at Antwerp and seize a French squadron which
was equipping there.   The plan was a very sound
one, but the expedition, known by the unhappy
name of Walcheren, was a failure, and may here
be dismissed once for all.   It must suffice to say
that, in spite of its miscarriage, it gave Napoleon
one of the worst frights of his life, and narrowly
missed bringing about a movement for his overthrow in Paris.

Let us now glance at the conditions in the
Iberian Peninsula.   No doubt if Napoleon had
been allowed to proceed with the subjugation of
Spain and Portugal methodically and opposed by
none except Spanish and Portuguese levies, he
might have succeeded in exacting some measure
of sullen submission.   But the whole population
held the French in abhorrence, and there was not

a man who would not cut a Frenchman's throat if
he had the chance; and the chances along a long
line of communications through a mountainous
country were many. It was unsafe for a French
officer to send a letter with a smaller escort than
five-and-twenty men, and a French straggler's life
was hardly worth an hour's purchase, for no
peasant would spare him. The French had attempted to put down this ferocity by reprisals—
hanging individuals and burning villages; but the
Spaniards had retorted by burning French soldiers
alive and sawing French officers asunder; and this
was a savagery which could not be outdone. The
insurgent spirit in the Peninsula was, in a word,
unquenchable except by extermination.

Moreover, methodical conquest had been prevented through the bold advance of Moore. He
had dislocated the whole of Napoleon's plans.
He had caused one hundred and twenty-five
thousand French soldiers to be hurried at desperate
and destructive speed in pursuit of his own forty
thousand, and had drawn some of them prematurely into distant regions before the intervening
territory had been systematically pacified. Then
Napoleon himself had returned to France, leaving his brother, King Joseph, at Madrid as

Commander-in-Chief; but none of the generals or marshals took the slightest heed of Joseph, first because they despised him as a civilian, and secondly because Napoleon sent them from his headquarters in Paris or elsewhere direct orders, frequently contradictory to Joseph's, over Joseph's head. Now from the configuration of the country in Spain, it would be difficult at the best of times not to allow subordinate commanders wide independence. Catalonia and the east coast, for instance, formed necessarily a distinct sphere of action. But when every commander of an army claimed the like independence, operations could not prosper. Napoleon had laid down in a general way that the greatest object of all was to hunt the British out of the Peninsula, and, if he had remained on the spot, he would no doubt have assembled, at all risks, men enough to accomplish this principal purpose. But it was beyond Joseph's power, not a little through Napoleon's own fault, to count upon any united effort of the generals who were nominally under his orders.

This discord between Joseph and the Marshals, and it may be added, among the Marshals themselves, was destined to prove of the first importance to Arthur Wellesley. It was everything for him to avert, if possible, any great concentration of French troops against himself. The two main roads for advance upon Lisbon from Spain lay, one to the north-east, by the Spanish frontier-fortress of Ciudad Rodrigo and the Portuguese of Almeida, and the other, a hundred miles farther to the south by the frontier-fortresses of Badajoz on the Spanish side and of Elvas on the Portuguese. We shall see that the more northerly of these was, for reasons which the map makes obvious, the route by which the principal French force always entered Portugal, and to which accordingly Wellesley devoted his personal attention. The danger constantly haunted him of a combined French movement by both routes; and thus we shall find him at the outset constantly in the vicinity of Almeida in person, with what may be called a flank-guard in the vicinity of Elvas, generally under the command either of Beresford or of Hill.

The other great advantage which he enjoyed was the security of his communications, guarded by the British Navy, between his advanced base at Lisbon and his fundamental base in England. Every British soldier and every ounce of British stores was carried easily and cheaply and safely (barring bad weather) by sea, without any molestation

whatever. Every French soldier had to walk, and
every ounce of French stores had to be carried from
France across the Pyrenees and for many score
of weary miles over bad and often mountainous
roads. The men wore out their boots, their clothing, and often their strength, they were liable to be
shot down by lurking patriots in any difficult de-
file, and certain of being assassinated if they fell
out. Wellesley did not contemplate a war of
attrition when he took command in 1809, but a
war of attrition his task proved to be; and the
British Navy then turned the scale of ordinary wear
and tear very heavily against the French.

So much for Wellesley's advantages: his disadvantages will presently appear, and we shall be
able to judge for ourselves how he triumphed over
the latter and turned the former to the utmost
account. Let us now very briefly note the dispositions made by Napoleon after the re-
embarkation of Moore's army. Soult, who had
hunted Moore to Coruña and received the surrender
of that place, was to turn southward upon Oporto
and Lisbon, Ney, who had taken part in the chase,
meanwhile clearing Galicia to north of him; while
Victor should second Soult's advance by a movement upon Lisbon westward along the valley of the

Guadiana, that is to say, by the route of Badajoz. When Wellesley arrived in the Tagus on the 22nd of April, he found that Soult, despite of a desperate resistance from the Spanish peasants, had reached Oporto and carried it by storm; while Victor, after completely defeating a Spanish army under General Cuesta at Medellin, was lying at Merida within less than forty miles of Badajoz and less than fifty of Elvas. Both were for the time halted, though there was nothing in front of Soult except some beaten Portuguese levies under General Silveira, nor of Victor, whose late opponent, Cuesta, was ruefully licking his wounds nearly fifty miles to south of him. Here, therefore, it may be said, there were preparing a frontal attack upon Lisbon from the north and a flank attack from the east; but there was no combination in the two movements. There was, in fact, no communication between the two Marshals, their headquarters being two hundred miles apart. Wellesley, therefore, was free to fall upon whichever of the two he might prefer.

He had ready to his hand some twenty-five thousand troops, British and of the German Legion, with thirty guns, for he had found it impossible to provide teams for more. These were distributed into divisions; four of infantry and one of cavalry; and this divisional organisation was maintained throughout the war. He had also some fifteen thousand Portuguese which General Beresford and other British officers had been licking into shape for the past six weeks, and which were daily improving. Transport was a great difficulty. His predecessor at Lisbon, Sir John Cradock, had tried in vain to collect mules, sending even to the Barbary coast for them; and Wellesley was obliged to fall back on the primitive ox-waggons of the country. He was also much hampered by the lack of ready-money, for Castlereagh had been unable to provide him with more than ten thousand pounds. England was very short of specie in those days; and the rate of exchange at Lisbon was twenty-five per cent. against her. His energy, however, overcame all obstacles; and he decided to advance northward against Soult, push him out of Portugal, and then, standing on the defensive in that quarter, to return and deal with Victor in co-operation with Cuesta. Meanwhile he laid hold of all the boats on the lower Tagus and left a force of twelve thousand British and Portuguese to watch Victor, in case of accidents. Finally, having concentrated his field-army at Coimbra, he started on the 7th of May for his march upon Oporto, himself taking the coast-road with the main body, and detaching Beresford with six thousand men to march by a parallel road farther east upon Viseu, so as to intercept the French retreat to eastward.

Soult, quite unaware of his intentions, had kept his army widely scattered, having a large body of cavalry and a division of infantry well south of Oporto. These detachments Wellesley tried to surprise and cut off; but his plans miscarried, and the French were able to retreat with little loss. On the 11th of May the British encamped about five miles south of the Douro, over against Oporto; but Soult had on the 8th been warned of his danger and had made all preparations for a retreat to eastward. He had only from ten thousand to twelve thousand men in Oporto, the rest of his troops being detached to northward; but he had resolved for various reasons not to move until the 12th, and having, as he thought, collected all the boats on the Douro, felt sure of several days respite before Wellesley could find the means to pass the river. Oporto is a city of cliffs, beneath which the Douro flows wide and deep, being then as yet unbridged. Behind such an obstacle Soult judged himself secure.

Early on the morning of the 12th a skiff was found by a British staff-officer on the south shore of the Douro. The owner pointed out four barges, unguarded, on the northern shore. These were brought over. Wellesley gave the order for the men to cross; and General Murray, whom we have met in India, was directed to take a small detachment of all three arms to a ferry, which was not damaged beyond repair, farther up the river. The barges were carrying over their third load of troops before the French took the alarm; but the British infantry had already fortified themselves strongly in a large isolated building, and could not easily be dislodged. The French General, Foy, hastily gathered together guns and infantry to attack it, but Wellesley also had his batteries in position. His first shrapnel shell dismounted the leading French gun as it was unlimbering, and disabled every man and horse belonging to it. The French gunners were driven from their pieces; the French infantry was repulsed with heavy loss from the building. As more and more British infantry crossed the river, they fell upon the flank of the assailants, and pressing on came upon the rear of Soult's main column, which was marching off to eastward. Soult then ordered a general retreat; but his rearguard was soon swept away, and the column became a mere disorderly mob. As such it streamed across the front of Murray, who had accomplished his crossing and taken up a position overlooking the road by which Soult's army must pass. Never had a man a better opportunity; but Murray, always irresolute, could not nerve himself to attack and destroy them, and allowed them to march on. The losses of the French amounted to six hundred killed, wounded, and prisoners; those of the British did not exceed one hundred and twenty-three. Wellesley had surprised a veteran enemy in broad daylight, and crossed a deep, broad and rapid river, with no more than a single boat at the outset, under Soult's very eyes.

Immediate pursuit was impossible owing to the necessary delay for bringing artillery, stores, and baggage across the river; but Beresford pushed on, and on the 13th Soult, learning that he lay across his line of retreat eastward at Amarante, realised that his only chance of escape was through the bleak mountains to northward. Perforce he destroyed his artillery, military chest, and baggage, and led his men by a very rough track into the valley of the Ave, making for Orense. Beresford and Silveira's Portuguese were hastening to cut off his retreat to east, Wellesley was following hard upon his track in rear; and only by desperate marches and after desperate perils did he reach Orense on the 19th. Though not pursued later than the 17th, he was fain, owing to lack of victuals, to hustle his troops on to Lugo, where he arrived on the 23rd with his army shoeless, and in many cases weaponless, in a state of utter exhaustion. The retreat had cost him six thousand men and all his artillery; and, had not Wellesley's pursuit been arrested on the 18th by the news of a movement of Victor on the Tagus, and Beresford's been slackened by the fatigue and hunger of his troops, it might have cost him the capture of himself and of the greater part of his army.

As things were, Wellesley returned southward to deal with Victor, and by the second week in June had assembled his whole force at Abrantes. He was by no means very happy in spite of his success. His men, though excellent in action, had behaved abominably on the march, and, owing to the trouble with regimental courts-martial, he found it hard to enforce discipline. He was short of money, he was short of horses, and he was short of transport-animals. The bullock-carts of the country were his abomination, for they were very slow at the best of times;[1] and there was hardly a road in Portugal that could be traversed except by pack-mules, which were almost unprocurable. However, reinforcements, including the famous Light Brigade trained by Moore at Shorncliffe, were on their way to him; and, as he now proposed to operate in Spain with the Spaniards, he threw himself chiefly on them to make good his needs. Now the Spaniards had set up a Central Provisional Government, called the Supreme Junta, which was now at Seville, and there were also local juntas in every province; but the trouble was that the authority of the Supreme Junta was not accepted and could not be enforced. They assured Wellesley that he should have everything for which he asked, and gave orders that it should be supplied; but there the matter ended, for no one took any notice of the orders. On paper everything was admirable, but on paper only. There was far too much jealousy among the local

---

[1] They still flourish, made wholly of wood, with axles that revolve with the wheels and make a lively creaking.

juntas, and between them and the Supreme Junta, to allow any transaction to go smoothly.

Happily such jealousy was not confined to them. Soult's arrival at Orense was the occasion of a bitter quarrel between him and Ney, whose campaign for the pacification of Galicia had failed rather ignominiously. Ney could hardly refuse to re-equip Soult's starving and demoralised men, but he did so grudgingly, reserving all comforts for his own soldiers. The result was such enmity between the two corps that there was danger of their engaging in a pitched battle. None were more bitter in the quarrel than Soult and Ney themselves; and matters came to a climax when they discussed future operations. Soult quoted Napoleon to the effect that the expulsion of the British was the first and principal object, and that Ney ought to help him to achieve it. Ney retorted that he had the Emperor's orders to clear Galicia, and that it was Soult's duty to assist him to do it. The contention grew so hot between the two Marshals that they nearly came to blows. Finally Soult gave in with a bad grace, but the only issue of their joint enterprise was that the French were driven for ever out of Galicia.

Meanwhile Victor remained supine about Merida,

without thought of interference with Cuesta's reorganisation of his army, until, having eaten up the country all round him, he begged leave to retreat to the Tagus. Joseph demurred until on the 10th of June he heard, not from Soult but from Paris, of the Marshal's disastrous retreat from Portugal, when he recalled Victor to Talavera and planned a general concentration of the corps within reach of him. This was a little difficult of accomplishment, since neither Soult nor Ney deigned to acquaint him with their movements; but nevertheless by the first week in July, through accident rather than design, Ney with the VIth Corps, Soult with the IInd, and Mortier with the Vth, together about fifty thousand men, had drifted to Astorga, Benavente, and Valladolid, positions from which they could descend, united within fourteen days upon the valley of the Tagus, where Victor lay. Joseph himself with a field-force of about ten thousand men was at Madrid, within four marches of Talavera, and yet another corps, the IVth, under General Sebastiani, seventeen thousand strong, was at Madridejos, about a hundred miles south-east of the same place. In little more than a fortnight, therefore, Joseph could assemble one hundred thousand men in the valley of the Tagus.

Such was the position when Wellesley with twenty-three thousand British joined Cuesta with about as many Spaniards at Plasencia, and agreed to march with him against Victor, who now lay behind the river Alberche, a little to east of Talavera. They supposed Soult and Ney to be fully occupied with operations in the north, and Sebastiani to have his hands full with a Spanish army, twenty-three thousand strong, under General Venegas, who lay to south of him and had orders to watch him. Mortier could be kept at bay by detaching a sufficient force to hold the pass of Baños, north of Plasencia, by which he must descend into the valley of the Tagus; but this, in spite of Wellesley's remonstrances, Cuesta declined to do. The whole march was one long story of wrangling and distress. Cuesta was not only old, obstinate, and incompetent, but so ill and feeble in body that he could neither walk nor ride, and was fain to follow his army in a lumbering coach drawn by nine mules. His army was without order, system, or discipline. Wellesley had been warned of this, but had not believed it. The promises of transport and supply were not fulfilled, and the British troops could never count upon their rations. Victor very imprudently gave his enemies the chance of overwhelming him on the river Alberche on the 24th of July; but Cuesta in spite of Wellesley's entreaties would not take it, though, when Victor retired, the old man became as rash as he had hitherto been cautious. Then on the 25th Joseph joined Victor with Sebastiani's corps and the troops from Madrid, making a total force of some forty-six thousand men; and Cuesta, who had been eager in pursuit, reluctantly retreated.

Wellesley had fortunately taken note of a position immediately to north of Talavera, and to this the allied army fell back on the 27th of July, steadily pressed by the French. The Spaniards were much shaken, and one British brigade of the rearguard allowed itself to be surprised and thrown into confusion. Wellesley extricated it in person, but, having done so, found himself obliged practically to take command of the Spaniards and place them on the ground allotted to them. The position which he had chosen was about three miles long, running northward from Talavera and the Tagus. The right, or southern, half of it was flat land and much enclosed, offering great advantages of defence; and a mile of this was assigned to the Spaniards. Beyond them the British occupied half a mile of the flat, then a mile of ridge. The

Spaniards were seized with panic while in the act of taking up their stations; four battalions took to their heels and disappeared; and Wellesley was fully employed in preventing the panic from spreading. The result was that he could not look to the disposition of his own troops; and, by some mistake, the key of the position on the summit of the ridge was left unoccupied.

Victor, observing this, made a dash to seize it after nightfall, but his plans went awry in the dark, and his columns after a sharp fight were repulsed, though at the cost of some four hundred casualties to the British. Wellesley then redistributed the troops as well as he could, and waited anxiously for the dawn of the 28th. He had not, as his despatch proves, by any means a correct idea of the disposition of the whole of his army even on the next day. The French commanders were determined to attack, but at variance as to the method; and Victor, taking matters into his own hands, launched at 5 a.m., under cover of a very heavy artillery fire, a division in close columns at the ridge held by the British. The assault was repulsed with heavy loss, nearly twelve hundred of the French being killed or wounded in forty minutes. There was then a lull. The day was intensely hot, and the soldiers of both armies went down and drank together of a brook that divided their arrays. After a time Joseph resolved to attack not only the ridge but the whole line of the British, containing the Spaniards, by a demonstration of his cavalry. The onslaught was delivered at 11.30 a.m. and after very severe fighting was repulsed, the British losing heavily because some of them in the ardour of success pushed a counter-attack too far and were driven back with heavy loss. Wellesley's keen eye foresaw the mishap, and he at once sent forward a brigade which saved the situation. Even after this second reverse Victor was trying for a third assault; but Joseph forbade it; and the French retired to their former position beyond the Alberche. They ought to have won the battle, for they had twice as many infantry as the British, and a greater weight of artillery, besides cavalry enough to overawe the Spaniards; but they lost it, chiefly through bad management and the insubordination of Victor, and sacrificed to no purpose seven thousand killed and wounded and seventeen guns.

Wellesley on his side had lost well over five thousand men in the two days' fighting, and on the 29th was unable to move. Craufurd's Light

Brigade joined him early in the morning; and he pressed Cuesta on the 30th in vain to advance, which the Spanish general, as events turned out, fortunately, declined to do. On the 1st of August came definite news that Soult had forced the pass of Baños with, as was reported, fourteen thousand men, and was descending into the valley of the Tagus. Wellesley then, with Cuesta's assent, turned back westward on the 3rd of August to attack him, and had reached Oropesa when he learned that Soult's force was twice as strong as he had supposed. It was evident that his retreat by the route of his forward march was cut off, so he filed his army to the south bank of the Tagus by the bridge of Arzobispo, leaving Cuesta, who was eager to fight, on the north bank. Good luck rather than good management saved Cuesta from annihilation; but meanwhile Wellesley's men and horses were starving, and the moral strength of the troops was seriously impaired. "With the army which a fortnight ago beat double their numbers," wrote Wellesley on the 8th of August, "I should now hesitate to meet a French corps of half their strength." Some days more were spent in angry wrangling with the Spanish generals, and on the 21st Wellesley decided to fall back to the Portu-

guese frontier by way of Badajoz, and to have
nothing more to do with them. At that time
neither men nor horses had had a full ration for a
month; the men were very sickly, and the horses
dying at the rate of one hundred a week. Altogether the close of the campaign was not cheering.
Wellesley had lost, apart from other casualties,
seven hundred of the men wounded in the battle,
having not carriage sufficient to take them away,
and the Spaniards, to whom he had entrusted his
captured guns, abandoned fourteen out of the
seventeen to the enemy. The only consolation,
though he was hardly aware of it, was that the
French were no better off than himself. In fact
the campaign of Talavera came to an end chiefly
because the various armies had to disperse in different directions in order to find something to eat.

There can, I think, be no doubt that Wellesley
in this advance into Spain took unwarrantable
risks, and that in fact he committed a serious mistake. But he should not be judged by wisdom
after the event. It was very important to take
the greatest possible advantage of the absence of
Napoleon and of his best troops in Austria; and,
after all, Sir Arthur had no experience to teach
him to distrust the Spaniards. He had, it must be

repeated, received warning not to count upon them, and had been informed of much that Moore had suffered at their hands; but no man is wholly free from vanity, and Arthur Wellesley was, perhaps, a little too anxious to show that he was a better man than Moore. It must, however, be remembered that Cuesta prevented him from striking hard at Victor before Joseph and Sebastiani joined him; that, if Venegas had done his duty, Joseph and Sebastiani would never have dared to move to Talavera; and that the rapid concentration of Soult's, Ney's, and Mortier's corps on his northern flank was the result of accident and not of design. But at any rate he had learned his lesson. "I have fished in many troubled waters," he said, "but Spanish troubled waters I will never fish in again."

He spent the remainder of the year at Badajoz, thinking deeply over the future. The Austrians, despite of some initial successes, had been heavily beaten at Wagram, and the armistice of Znaim, concluded on the 12th of July, had, owing to the failure of the Walcheren expedition, been confirmed by the Peace of Vienna signed on the 14th of October. Austria, therefore, had for the present withdrawn from the struggle, and Napoleon and his best troops would be set free for work in the Peninsula in 1810. What was to be done? After much consideration Wellesley adhered to his original opinion that Portugal could still be defended, and Lisbon, at any rate, held; and he set his chief engineer to construct fortified lines from the sea to the estuary of the Tagus above Torres Vedras, some thirty or forty miles north of the capital. If he could retain no more than this little space, with the all-important port of Lisbon, he could still make the French tenure of the Peninsula insecure. It needed a man of long sight to perceive this, but Wellesley saw it, and never for a moment lost heart.

Meanwhile the reigning administration in England had fallen and given place to a new one under Spencer Perceval, for which everyone predicted a short life. This Ministry backed Wellesley loyally, created him Viscount Wellington for his victory at Talavera, and after a desperate battle in Parliament carried a vote of thanks to him for his services. There was much adverse comment on the campaign, which certainly was in many points open to criticism; and a deal of appalling nonsense was talked in both Houses of Parliament by noble lords and gentlemen of the Opposition, with lapses from good taste which are almost incredible. Both in the Lords and Commons men were found, who, safe under the shelter of Parliamentary privilege, uttered the base and cowardly insinuation that Wellington had fought the Battle of Talavera in order to win a peerage. As a matter of fact, Wellington was struck during the action by a spent bullet, which, if it had possessed but a little more velocity, would have sent him to his grave an irredeemable commoner. But faction breeds vulgarity as surely as dirt breeds flies. At any rate the Ministers stood by him, and Lord Liverpool, the new Secretary for War, sent him more reinforcements than he had asked for. He could, therefore, afford to despise the hysterical clamour of hungry Whigs.

Christmas was still some weeks distant when the Spaniards embarked, as their manner was, in a mad winter campaign in Central Spain, which presently issued in the crushing defeat of Areizaga, Cuesta's successor, on the 19th of November at Ocaña. This was lamentable, and yet out of it came good. Joseph, abetted by Soult, turned his victory to the most foolish and, so far as his master Napoleon was concerned, most undutiful account that was possible. Instead of keeping their attention fixed upon the British Army which, as the Emperor had insisted, was the only danger in the Peninsula, they invaded Andalusia, the richest and most populous province in Spain, less for military reasons than in the hope of filling their pockets and living a comfortable life. Wellington could hardly believe the news when he heard it; such madness seemed it to him for a general to spread an army, already insufficient to hold the ground which it had gained, over a still greater area of rebellious country. Yet of this madness Joseph and Soult were guilty; and, worse than this, though they overran the province with ease, they failed, through sheer carelessness, to master Cadiz before a Spanish force had thrown itself into the city and prepared to defend it. Andalusia without Cadiz was like Portugal without Lisbon; and Cadiz, once missed, was thenceforward impregnable. It is by nature the most inaccessible of places by land, and could not be taken by force except with the help of a naval armament which France, owing to Britain's supremacy at sea, could not hope to provide. The Supreme Junta, which had removed from Seville to Cadiz, upon the approach of the French army, begged Wellington for troops to aid in the defence. He gladly sent them three battalions and two batteries which Liverpool presently augmented by reinforcements from home to a total strength of eight thousand men under Sir Thomas Graham. Nothing could better have pleased Wellington than to see large bodies of French troops distracted from the invasion of Portugal to a perfectly hopeless task.

Napoleon, meanwhile, had collected one hundred and thirty-eight thousand men for a final effort in the Peninsula, and, by the end of February 1810, though the whole of these reinforcements had not yet crossed the French frontier, he had nearly three hundred thousand men in Spain. But he was, naturally and rightly, much annoyed by Joseph's entry into Andalusia, and punished his brother by depriving him of practically all military, and nearly all civil, authority. He wanted the spoil of Spain to swell his own revenues, and not to pay for Joseph's kingly extravagances. He then sent Massena, the ablest of all his Marshals, to take independent command of an Army of Portugal, which was composed of the IInd, VIth, and VIIIth Corps, and placed Soult in the like control of the Ist, IVth, and Vth Corps, as the Army of Andalusia. With three corps, counting in all some sixty-five thousand men, he doubted not that

Massena would succeed in driving the British from Portugal.

Wellington, for his part, was wrestling with many difficulties, the chief of which was want of cash; but his Commissariat was improving, and he had managed to obtain some mules from Tangier. Most carefully he thought out the problem of the defence of Portugal. It was most unlikely that the French would enter the country south of the Tagus, but he was obliged to provide against the chance; and so he left a British division and the bulk of the Portuguese regulars under General Rowland Hill about Abrantes and Thomar. The space between the Tagus and the Douro, about one hundred miles, is cut in two by the impassable barrier of the Serra da Estrella; and, since the southern portion of this space was an unlikely point of entrance, it was entrusted to the Portuguese militia, while the northern portion, being the most vulnerable, he occupied himself with eighteen thousand British and fourteen thousand Portuguese. These were assembled in the dreary, bleak, barren corner of the Portuguese Highlands that lies between Pinhel, Almeida, Guarda, and Celorico.

The French were late in getting to work, and

did not begin their first operation—the siege of the Spanish frontier-fortress of Ciudad Rodrigo— until the 15th of June. The place surrendered, after twenty-six days of open trenches, on the 10th of July; and on the 21st Massena pushed Ney's corps across the boundary upon Almeida. In this quarter Wellington had posted the Light Division under General Robert Craufurd as a corps of observation, with strict orders not to venture upon a serious engagement. Craufurd was the best trainer of troops in the army, but was uncertain as a commander in the field. Moreover, he was a man with a grievance. He was five years older than Wellington, but, having abjured military duty for a time to engage himself in some mercantile speculation, which failed, he could only resume it with some loss of seniority. Hence he was discontented with his lot and morbidly anxious to retrieve his blunder by distinguished service; and, being both jealous and ill-tempered, he was constantly intriguing against Wellington and trying to put himself forward. His favourite method was to engage himself in unnecessary affairs of outposts; and on this occasion, when Ney advanced with twenty-five thousand men, Craufurd had the audacity to await him and fight him on the

[147]

23rd with one fourth of Ney's numbers on the river Coa. Handling his division very badly he was saved from disaster by the skill of his regimental officers and the superb behaviour of his troops, but he lost three hundred killed and wounded and endangered the whole of his division for no useful purpose whatever. Wellington was greatly annoyed, but said little, for he knew that, in so uncertain a game as war, a chief must not be extreme to mark what is done amiss by zealous subordinates. "If I am to be hanged for it," he wrote to his brother after this affair, "I cannot accuse a man who, I believe, has served well, and whose error is one of judgment and not of intention; and indeed I must add that, although my errors and those of others also are visited heavily upon me, that is not the way in which any, much less a British, army can be commanded." These words might with advantage be writ large in the offices of our great Ministers of State, who are apt to demand a military scapegoat to bear the blame of any military mishap, and are specially swift to find one when the fault is directly attributable to themselves.

After the action of Coa, which cost the French five hundred casualties, there followed for Welling-

ton a month of suspense, with distracting reports of
French movements in all directions, and a troublesome quarrel with the Portuguese Government in
Lisbon; but at last on the 15th of August Ney laid
siege to Almeida. Wellington at once made dispositions to straiten the quarters of the enemy as
much as possible so as to render subsistence difficult, and reckoned that Almeida might well detain
the enemy for two months. An accidental explo-
sion within the fortress, however, compelled its
surrender within a week, and Wellington, much
disappointed, made all preparations against an
immediate advance of the French. Yet there was
still more delay. Massena, like all of Napoleon's
generals, lived on the country; and the country,
thanks to Wellington's precautions, was bare. It
took the Marshal long to collect a fortnight's
provisions, and even then he had to sacrifice
artillery-horses to carry them; but at last on the
15th of September he started with his three corps—
the IInd (Reynier), the VIth (Ney), and the
VIIth (Junot)—and abandoning his communications marched upon Lisbon.

Massena, though no more than fifty-two years of
age, was prematurely old and worn out through
the hardships of many campaigns. He had ac-

cepted his present command unwillingly, and being, though a military genius, of low character, worked ill with his colleagues. Ney and he were old enemies; Junot was furious at being superseded by him as supreme over the army of Portugal; Reynier he disliked. He had little knowledge of the country, and was provided with the worst of maps.[1] For information he depended mainly upon a few individuals of the French party in Portugal. Misled by these, Massena took the worst high road in Portugal, north of the Serra da Estrella, upon Coimbra, and then struck south. Wellington retired before him with perfect steadiness and order until he reached the Serra de Bussaco, some ten miles north of that city. This lofty and isolated ridge, about ten miles along and eighteen hundred feet high, towers above the surrounding broken country like a giant; and here Wellington resolved to stand and fight for southern Portugal. He was aware that the position could be turned, but hoped either that the turning movement might be parried by some of his irregular troops, or that a successful general action might suffice for his purpose. He had summoned Hill's division to him, which raised his

[1] The actual map that he used was most kindly lent to me for a time by the Library of the University of Belfast.

strength to fifty thousand good troops; and though, even so, he could not properly occupy nine miles of front, he had made a road on the reverse side of the ridge by which his troops could move rapidly to any threatened point. He drew up his line, likewise, as was his invariable practice on the reverse side of the slope, so that they could not be seen, and so he awaited with confidence the coming attack.

Massena was not the man to shrink from a battle. He was aware that Wellington's British troops did not exceed thirty thousand, reckoned that not even all of these could be present, and he knew nothing of the Portuguese, now, thanks to British training, converted into good infantry. Having sixty thousand men of his own, he, on the 27th of September, threw them confidently against the steep ascent without proper reconnaissance and without a thought that he could give them no support with his artillery. It takes an active, unladen man three-quarters of an hour to climb from the bottom of Bussaco hill to the top; and it must have taken the French columns twice as long. When at last they did reach the summit, panting and breathless, they were easily shattered and driven down with heavy loss; and Massena was fain to accept repulse, having lost forty-six hundred killed and wounded, whereas Wellington's casualties did not exceed twelve hundred and fifty. Taking the regiments actually under fire only, on both sides, twenty-six thousand French were easily beaten by fifteen thousand British and Portuguese.

Reeling under this buffet, Massena on the night of the 28th turned the ridge of Bussaco, as he might have done without fighting, and continued his advance, while Wellington retreated before him. Having sacked Coimbra from cellar to garret, the Marshal left there forty-five hundred sick and wounded, with only one hundred and forty men to guard them, and on the 4th of October pressed on. Within less than a week of his departure the whole of the forty-five hundred had been captured and carried off by a body of Portuguese irregulars which was following up the line of his march. On the 10th of October the British retired within the lines of Torres Vedras, and on the 14th Massena in person came up to reconnoitre with amazement and dismay. Detailed description of the lines would be too lengthy for this place; but it may be said that the country between Torres Vedras and Lisbon resembles nothing so much as a gigantic mountain-torrent suddenly converted into solid rock, and that cunning advantage had been taken of every peak, gully, and ravine. The Marshal turned in fury upon his Portuguese intelligencers, and asked why they had not informed him of these details. They stammered out that they did not know of all the defences that the British had thrown up. "Hang it, they didn't throw up these mountains," answered the Marshal. In deep dudgeon he examined the lines on the following days, satisfied himself that he could not force them, and then sending a trusted officer to lay the whole situation before Napoleon, he halted his army and sat down. Before long the greater part of his force was dispersed in all directions in search of food and forage. Farther and farther they went afield, and scanter and scantier grew the supplies. At length after a month's stay the Marshal was driven by sheer starvation to retreat, and on the 14th of November he began to fall back some thirty miles north-eastward to Santarem.

Cautiously Wellington followed him up, the route of the French being marked by the corpses of starved animals and soldiers, and sat down in his turn. There was no occasion for him to attack. He had his transport and supply system in fairly good order by this time and could wait indefinitely, whereas Massena was bound to move as soon as he had exhausted the country. It was an anxious time for Wellington. The Government at home was weak, and might on any day be driven from office by a new administration which—such is faction—would at once have withdrawn the army from the Peninsula. Massena knew this too, and clung to his ground in confidence that the Whig party would banish all his difficulties for him. December passed away, and in January Wellington heard bad news from the east. Napoleon, on receiving Massena's messenger, had directed the IXth Corps, under d'Erlon, to move down to Coimbra from the north, and Soult with the Vth Corps (Mortier), and other troops—twenty thousand in all,—to leave his comfortable quarters at Cadiz and move upon Portugal south of the Tagus, to make a diversion in Massena's favour. Accordingly, in the middle of January, 1811, Soult arrived at Badajoz; and five weeks later the Spanish army which was on the spot to watch him, obligingly gave itself up to be utterly beaten. Wellington was furious, for the Spanish general had done everything which Wellington had particularly begged him not to do; and this was the result. He pushed the Second Division, ten battalions, under

Beresford, to the other side of the Tagus, about Salvaterra, to guard against this new menace from the east, and devoted all his energies to the penning of Massena within the smallest possible area. But meanwhile d'Erlon's arrival with eight thousand men at Leiria, some forty miles north-west of Santarem, had kept the Portuguese irregulars at a distance and widened Massena's feeding-ground a little. February passed away and March came in, but still the obstinate Marshal held his ground. He laid trap after trap to induce Wellington to attack him, which Wellington knew far better than to do, but beyond this he made no motion. He had lingered two months longer than Wellington had thought possible; but still he would not go.

At last, on the 5th of March, Wellington observed signs of movement among the French, and closed up his divisions in readiness to advance. As a matter of fact, Massena, manœuvring for concealment with admirable skill, had begun his retreat on the 3rd; and by the 7th his army was safely aligned between Leiria and Thomar. Wellington followed him up, obtaining contact with his rearguard on the 10th; and from that day there were little actions almost daily. French writers are disposed to deride Wellington for his extreme caution at the outset of the pursuit; but he was obtaining his will, and there was no occasion for him to risk even a small reverse by excessive temerity. Ney was a master in handling a rearguard, and Massena was never so dangerous as when really in difficulties. On the 14th Massena decided to hasten his retirement, and gave orders to destroy all baggage, the bulk of his wheeled vehicles, and all worn-out animals; but on the 15th at Foz d'Arouce two of his divisions were within a hair's-breadth of a disastrous rout, and his casualties numbered four hundred. Demoralisation was evidently setting in among Massena's troops, but just at this time there came bad news to Wellington from the east. Badajoz had been treacherously surrendered to Soult on the 10th, and it was imperatively necessary to reinforce Beresford at once. At a stroke he had to reduce his force from forty-four thousand to thirty-eight thousand men; but reinforcements sufficient to make good this detachment had recently landed at Lisbon, and he was still able to continue the chase. By this time Massena, Ney, Junot, and Reynier were all pulling different ways, and the French army was almost in a state of mutiny. Ney, hotly disputing one of Massena's orders, was by him deprived of his command and sent back to Spain. D'Erlon, pleading Napoleon's orders, likewise retired to Spain, and took the IXth Corps with him; and Reynier was difficult and insubordinate. On the 3rd of April, Reynier's corps, left in isolation at Sabugal, only through a succession of accidents, due chiefly to a dense fog, escaped utter destruction, and suffered four times as many casualties as the British. So the retreat continued with ever-increasing misery and disorder. By the 8th of April the whole of Massena's army had crossed the Portuguese frontier, half-starved, more than half barefooted, and with clothing in rags; and the retirement did not end until it reached Salamanca. Massena's campaign had cost him twenty-five thousand men, of whom two thousand had fallen in action, eight thousand were prisoners, and fifteen thousand had perished from sickness and famine. The great French invasion of 1810 had been brought to naught.

It was a moment of triumph, but Wellington had no heart to enjoy it. His generals during the pursuit had for the most part shown incapacity, and he had been obliged to do everything himself. He had been, as he said, "general of the cavalry and of the advanced guard, and leader of two or three columns, sometimes all on the same day." Again, the Portuguese Government was neglecting its army shamefully; and even the British Government seemed to Wellesley, though he misjudged them, to be none too staunch to the cause. Moreover, that Government appeared too weak to last; and he sickened at the thought that all the sacrifices which the Portuguese had made at his appeal might, through the faction of vain men at Westminster, have been offered in vain. The prospects of the future seemed dark; and very sorrowfully he made all arrangements for the re-embarkation of his army, lest the worst should befall. He knew that he had done his best and that he had accomplished much by foresight, constancy, and patience; yet the vote of a few politicians, likely enough too much bemused with wine to know rightly what they were doing, might wreck everything.

Yet in truth, though he knew it not, Portugal had been virtually freed from the French for ever; and he had learned the secret of driving them from Spain also. He had only to show himself on the Spanish border with forty thousand men, and with his service for transport and supply fully organised to keep them fed, and the French must at once assemble fifty thousand to meet him. Every district weakened by the concentration of those fifty

thousand men was at once beset, not so much by the
Spanish armies, as by guerilla-bands, which patriot-
ism had called into being, under very able leaders,
to supersede those armies. These bands had not
yet attained to their full strength, but were becoming steadily more formidable. They harried columns on the march, overwhelmed and destroyed
isolated posts, cut off and slew small parties, des-
patch-riders and stragglers. Meanwhile, the fifty
thousand, living on the country, could not stay
long in one place. Massena, by immense strength
of will, had remained at Santarem for nearly four
months, but his men had been compelled to wander
fifty or sixty miles away to find food, and vast numbers had perished. Sooner or later the fifty thousand must move forward or back. If they offered
him an advantage, Wellington could fight them; if
not, he could retire and play once more the game
that he had played with Massena. If only the
British Government would stand by him, it was only
a question of time and patience before the French
must be driven from the Peninsula. Should Napoleon entangle himself in other wars, the time
would be shorter; should he be able to devote all
of his energies to Spain, it would be longer. But,
looking to the insurgent spirit of the Spaniards,

there was a prospect that even Napoleon in person might fail to subdue it; and, if he should suffer reverses, all Europe would soon rise up against him. For years he had been playing double or quits, and so far his luck had tided him through all; but if luck turned against him, his shrift would be short. Wellington had taken the measure not only of the French armies but of the Emperor, and, amid all disappointments, he never lost confidence.

CHAPTER V

THE first comfortable news that came to Wellington in March 1811 was that Soult had returned hastily from Badajoz to Andalusia on the 13th, leaving Mortier with eleven thousand men to hold the captured fortress. During Soult's absence the British and Spanish troops in Cadiz had seized the moment to attack the besieging force and had gained a signal victory at Barrosa. The success, thanks to the apathy of the Spanish general, had not been turned to the best account; but that was perhaps no disadvantage, for the raising of the siege of Cadiz would have liberated more French troops for work in the field than might have been agreeable to Wellington. However, since Soult had run back with a great part of his force, Wellington directed Beresford with two brigades of cavalry, two divisions of British and one of Portuguese infantry, to move down to Badajoz and lay siege to it. After one or two brilliant affairs with the French cavalry on his way, Beresford found himself free to beleaguer the fortress, before which Wellington in person joined him on the 22nd of

[161]

April. He felt sure that Soult would presently return from Andalusia to relieve the threatened place, and, in that event, he authorised Beresford to fight or fall back, as he might think best. This done, he returned to his own army, the headquarters of which lay just across the Spanish frontier, ten miles west of Ciudad Rodrigo, where it had abandoned the pursuit of Massena. It was engaged in covering the blockade of the adjoining fortress of Almeida.

Massena, meanwhile, had been trying to make good the defects of his army at Salamanca, by no means with the goodwill of Bessières, who was in command of the district. Massena had hoped for a reinforcement of eight to ten thousand men; but Bessières seemed to think that he fulfilled all his duty to his colleague by bringing him seventeen hundred men and his noble self. However, being anxious to save Almeida, Massena, on the 2nd of May, crossed the Agueda with forty-eight thousand men and thirty-eight guns; and Wellington, being equally anxious to take Almeida and at the same time to strengthen the British Government's hands by a successful action, resolved to meet him on the extreme western edge of the great plain of Leon. He had no more than thirty-seven thousand men, twenty-five thousand of them British, and forty-eight guns, having, as we have seen, strengthened Beresford in order to enable him to meet Soult. He was, in fact, about to take the very great risk of fighting two pitched battles, one with his flank-guard, and one with his main body, weakening the latter so as to strengthen the former, and leaving both really in insufficient force. And the risk was the greater since he was greatly inferior to Massena in cavalry. But one sign of a great commander is to know when he may take liberties; and he reckoned that Massena's army, after its late humiliating experience, would not be in the best of heart, nor its leaders in the best of accord.

His chosen position lay behind some eight miles of deep ravine, shallow to the south, where he had rested his right on the village of Fuentes de Oñoro, but rapidly deepening as it runs north. Massena perceived at once that this village was the key of the position, and on the 3rd of May he made an isolated attack upon it with one division; but after a sharp fight he was beaten off with heavy loss, his casualties numbering six hundred and fifty against the British two hundred and fifty. Spending the next day in careful reconnaissance, he perceived that Wellington's right beyond the village was unprotected, and made his dispositions to turn that flank. Wellington, realising their purport, took such counter-measures as his numbers permitted; but, when the French renewed their attack on the 5th, he could not foil the turning movement and was fain to throw his right wing back in the full heat of action. This manœuvre should have been impossible if the French divisional generals had seconded their leader and each other loyally, and had handled their troops with skill; but the Light Division under Robert Craufurd, backed by the cavalry under Stapleton Cotton, accomplished it with admirable steadiness and devotion, and so saved the day. By sheer discipline and endurance they held at bay great masses of French cavalry; and when Massena, confident of his success against the British right, again assaulted Fuentes de Oñoro, he was beaten back after savage fighting with bloody losses. After this failure he broke off the action, and, though he remained on his ground until the night of the 7th, he then retreated, leaving Almeida to its fate. His casualties did not exceed twenty-two hundred against Wellington's fifteen hundred and thirty, but he saw no prospect of success. In truth, the French troops did not fight well, showing little of their usual dash and courage in attack; and on this Wellington seems to have counted, for with a position so defective he undoubtedly took almost unwarrantable risks. His own comment on the action was, "If Boney had been there, we should have been beat." He was lucky to escape defeat, and he knew it. But Massena, though a very great soldier, was not Bonaparte, and Wellington knew that too.

He now straitened the blockade of Almeida, the fall of which in a few days was certain; but to his infinite mortification, the garrison, owing to the blunders of several British officers, contrived to blow up the fortress, to slip away on the night of the 10th, and to rejoin Massena with three-fourths of its numbers. Wellington was furious over this wretched affair, and vented his wrath in terms so scathing that one unfortunate officer shot himself. On that same day came a message from the Emperor at Paris, superseding Massena in the command of the army of Portugal, by Marmont, Duke of Ragusa; and from henceforward Massena disappears from our view. Wellington always declared without hesitation that he was the ablest opponent that he had to meet in the Peninsula, and that Massena was always in the place where he least wanted to find him. When the two men met many years afterwards, Massena told Wellington that he had turned every hair in his body grey, to which Wellington answered that things had been pretty evenly divided between them. Beyond all doubt Wellington was relieved to see the last of Massena.

Marmont at once withdrew the army to Salamanca, being unable to feed it where it lay, and Wellington's attention was now distracted to Beresford. The siege of Badajoz had not prospered owing to want of skilled engineers and of proper material, for though Wellington's own siege-train was floating in Lisbon harbour, he had never yet ventured to land it. Moreover, as Wellington had anticipated, Soult was hastening back from Seville with twenty-four thousand men and fifty guns to relieve the fortress; and Beresford's letters had so uncomfortable a sound that Wellington on the 16th of May decided to join his subordinate in person at once. He arrived too late. On the 16th Beresford, with eight thousand British and twenty-one thousand Spaniards under Generals Blake and Castaños, had marched out to meet Soult at Albuera, the place chosen for him by Wellington, and had made a sad mess of the battle. He had occupied the position wrongly, and handled his troops

with doubtful skill. In fact he had thought that
he was beaten and ordered a retreat; and he would
have been beaten had not Captain Henry Hardinge, of his staff, taken it upon himself to win
the day. Four thousand of his eight thousand
British had fallen, besides three thousand Spaniards; and he would have written a "whining report" and ruined everything, had not Wellington
come up in the nick of time to explain to him that
he had won a victory. Soult, having lost at least
eight thousand men, retired once more to Seville,
leaving several hundred wounded men behind him.
Thus the crisis was past. The advance of the
French in the north to save Almeida and in the
east to save Badajoz had been repelled by two general actions. It was a great feat to have accomplished by judicious handling of forty thousand
British soldiers.

Now then, was the time to secure the frontier of
Portugal permanently by the capture of Badajoz
and Ciudad Rodrigo. Marmont would need weeks
to re-equip and reorganise his army. Soult had retired to a safe distance at Usagre, ninety miles to
southeast of Badajoz; d'Erlon had been ordered
back to join Soult in Andalusia by Napoleon.
Wellington posted troops to keep Soult under ob-

servation, and with fourteen thousand British and Portuguese sat down to the siege of Badajoz. Time was an object, for Soult was certain to move to its relief as soon as d'Erlon should have joined him, and Marmont likewise was not likely to remain long supine at Salamanca. It was, therefore, decided to prosecute the siege as before with bad Portuguese cannon; and the operations consequently did not prosper. After a fortnight of open trenches Wellington on the 10th of June raised the siege, for Marmont had marched, on the 6th, south-eastward by the pass of Baños to join Soult; and for the second time an invasion of Portugal was to be attempted, not by two independent columns acting without concert, but by a single united army.

Wellington thereupon concentrated his forces from Portugal and from the neighbourhood of Badajoz on the river Caia, to north-west of that fortress, and on the 17th of June, Marmont effected his junction with Soult at Merida, some thirty miles to eastward. The two Marshals were on cordial terms, and with nearly sixty thousand men advanced joyfully upon their enemy. Wellington could match against them thirty-seven thousand British and seventeen thousand Portuguese, or fifty-four thousand men in all. On the 23rd Soult and Marmont made a reconnaissance in force, but gained thereby little knowledge of Wellington's position or numbers; and on the following day Soult made an excuse for returning with his army to Seville. The truth seems to be that he was not anxious at that moment to meet the British again. He had been roughly handled by Beresford at Albuera, and might fare even worse if encountered by Wellington. Marmont protested vehemently, and, having but twenty-eight thousand men of his own, insisted that Soult must leave fifteen thousand of the army of Andalusia with him. The request was so reasonable that Soult gave way, though with ill grace, and on the 28th he marched off with the remainder of his men, the two Marshals parting finally, as was natural, on friendly terms. So the moment of peril for Wellington passed almost with mockery away. Marmont waited over against him for a few weeks in order to cover the revictualling of Badajoz, and then retired on the 13th of July to the valley of the Tagus. Wellington thereupon drew his troops into cantonments covering the eastern frontier of Portugal from the Tagus southward to the Guadiana.

But he had no intention of remaining for long idle. The Spaniards, excepting the guerilla-leaders, had not taken such advantage as he had hoped of the concentration of Soult's and Marmont's forces against him, which was a disappointment; but, on the other hand, he was conscious that the initiative was passing from the French commanders to himself. He now at last landed his siege-train, and leaving the defence of the eastern frontier to Sir Thomas Graham, who had taken the place of Beresford absent on sick-leave, he marched himself with two divisions and a brigade of cavalry for the Agueda. By the 11th of August he held Ciudad Rodrigo under blockade; and Marmont, raising his army to fifty-eight thousand men by drawing troops from General Dorsenne in the north, marched to its relief. Wellington brought up additional divisions to the number of thirty thousand British and sixteen thousand Portuguese, towards the threatened place, without uniting them into a single body; and they were still thus dispersed when, on the 25th of September, Marmont made a reconnaissance in strong force. The result was a lively little combat at El Bodon, where Wellington, though greatly outnumbered and for some time in considerable danger, withdrew a small isolated force with great skill, inflicting more damage than he received. In fact he took great liberties with Marmont, who, jealous of his own reputation, was too cautious to turn his opponent's temerity to account. Falling back after this combat to a very strong position Wellington offered Marmont battle; but the Marshal was not to be tempted, and on the 1st of October he retired once more to his cantonments in the Tagus, while Wellington went into winter-quarters thirty miles west of Ciudad Rodrigo. The campaign was closed by a successful spring by General Hill, who had been left with about sixteen thousand men at Portalegre, to watch d'Erlon's corps in Estremadura, upon an isolated French detachment at Arroyo Molinos, some seventy miles to eastward. In this affair about two thousand French were killed or captured, at a cost of no more than one hundred casualties to Hill—a very welcome little success.

And now Napoleon, being bent upon his coming invasion of Russia, changed his plans in Spain. General Suchet had been successful in the eastern provinces; and the Emperor resolved to reinforce him from Marmont's army, first to subdue Valencia and Andalusia thoroughly, and then turn the united strength of his forces upon Portugal. The plan was not a bad one in itself, but did not make good the vital defect of the French armies in Spain—lack of unity in command. The Emperor had provided Joseph with an efficient chief of staff in the person of Jourdan; but, if the subordinate generals would not report their movements to him, his efficiency could be of no great profit. Wellington on his side, despite of much sickness in his army, was determined to besiege and capture Ciudad Rodrigo, and so to close the north-eastern gate of Portugal to the French for ever. He had by this time made his army into a fairly handy instrument. The organisation of pack-mules for transport was approaching perfection. His staff, with experience, had grown far more capable; and his system of intelligence was excellent. He had the great advantage over the French that both Spaniards and Portuguese gave every information to him and withheld it from the enemy; and he had officers of extraordinary linguistic powers, audacity, and resource, who possessed a perfect genius for penetrating the secrets of the French. In the field, British officers, mounted on thoroughbred horses, surveyed the French columns placidly from a distance of a few hundred yards, secure in the certainty that no French horse had the speed to catch them. Altogether the moral quality of the army was greatly improved, not least by an unbroken chain of successes.

On the 1st of January 1812 Wellington issued his orders for the approach to Ciudad Rodrigo, and, having posted Hill with a sufficient force in his old station between Portalegre and Castello Branco, to check any French advance from Andalusia and Estremadura, he on the 8th invested the fortress. Marmont's troops were scattered in all directions to find subsistence—the usual condition of an army which lives on the country,—and the Marshal himself was travelling from Talavera to Valladolid. He heard nothing of the siege until the 15th, by which time Wellington had long been master of the principal points of vantage; and he could only order a hasty concentration by forced marches from all quarters. Before he could move from Valladolid, he heard to his consternation that Ciudad Rodrigo had fallen on the 19th. Having too few mortars and howitzers to silence the guns of the fortress, Wellington had contented himself with laying open the walls, and, having made his breach, had stormed the place out of hand. The losses from the enemy's artillery during the siege had exceeded five hundred, and in the assault, where Craufurd fell mortally wounded, had numbered nearly as many more; and it may be that, with more scientific management and better material of war, the casualties might have been greatly reduced and the fortress might have surrendered without an assault. But this would have taken time; and here was the astonishing fact that Wellington had in twelve days mastered a stronghold which, even when defended by a few thousand Spanish levies, had defied Ney for twenty-five. Marmont was so utterly staggered by the blow that he could only sit still and gasp; for within the fortress lay the only means for its recapture, the French siege-train. Wellington made up his mind that there was nothing now to prevent him from besieging the other main stronghold on the Portuguese border, Badajoz. Meanwhile, he dispersed his army innocently into cantonments. Marmont did likewise. The Marshal indeed had no choice. He could not keep his army concentrated because he had no accumulation of supplies, and for the same reason he was unable to cross the exhausted country—until the next harvest a mere waste—which lay between him and Wellington. So helpless is an army which lives on such falsehoods as Napoleon's contemptuous phrase:

"Supplies; not a word to me about supplies![1]
Twenty thousand men can live in a desert."

After no more than a month's respite Wellington began his movement on the 16th of February,
learning on the way that he had been promoted to
an earldom for the capture of Ciudad Rodrigo.
He himself took charge of the siege, while Hill
advanced to Merida to cover the leaguer against
any possible French advance from the Tagus.
The place was invested and ground was broken on
the 17th of March, and by the 5th of April the
engineers reported that the batteries had laid open
a practicable breach. Wellington, thereupon, ordered the assault to be delivered on the 6th. Time
was precious, for Soult was advancing to the relief
of the fortress, and this was the excuse for Wellington's haste, for the defences had not yet been
battered adequately, and such damage as had been
done had been made good by the brave and
energetic French commander. The result was
that in spite of desperate efforts and hideous
slaughter every attempt to storm by the main
breach failed, and the place was finally taken by the
escalade of the castle. A member of Wellington's
staff has recorded that the two hours spent with him

[1] Les vivres! Ne m'en parlez pas!

during the assault were the most miserable that he ever passed. Report after report of failure came in, and Wellington remained calm and unmoved. Then came a final hopeless report, and his jaw dropped; but with perfect calm he sent orders to Picton, who had already failed once to scale the castle wall, to try again. Picton had already done so of his own motion, and when the news of his success came in, the staff burst into a cry of exultation, but Wellington never moved a muscle of his face. Only next day when he saw the pile of red-coated corpses in the breach did his fortitude desert him, and he burst into a passion of tears.

Having gained possession of the city, the troops gave themselves up wholly to drunkenness and pillage; and though Wellington, furiously angry, fulminated orders, he could not stop the riot for three full days. Some five thousand British and Portuguese fell in the assault, while French writers claim that not twenty of the defenders were killed or hurt. Wellington was too much accustomed to the rough-and-ready methods of assailing Indian fortresses to appreciate the skill and resource which a brave, scientific and energetic commander could bring to bear upon the defence. However, Badajoz was taken, and the troops, for all their indiscipline upon the immediate fall of the fortress, showed an obstinacy and devotion in the attack which has hardly a parallel in the history of the army.

Meanwhile Marmont had advanced, at the end of March, upon Ciudad Rodrigo with twenty-six thousand men, and, owing to the temerity of the commander whom Wellington had left upon the spot, was able to advance much further than he should have been permitted to do. But the Marshal, in difficulties as usual over his supplies, was presently obliged to disperse his troops, and upon Wellington's advance to meet him, he fell back to Salamanca, and placed his troops in cantonments, keeping them as closely assembled as the means of subsistence would permit. Soult, who had been detained in Andalusia by false reports and feint movements of an advance of the British to attack him, likewise cantoned his troops, being paralysed for the present by want of provisions. Wellington therefore followed their example. His spring campaign had been brilliantly successful, for he had not only mastered Ciudad Rodrigo and Badajoz, but had taken in the one the French siege-train and in the other the French pontoon-train, thus depriving the enemy of the means of recapturing

[177]

the lost fortresses and of their facilities for passing rivers. He now detached Hill to destroy the French bridge of boats at Almaraz, a service which was executed after a brilliant little action on the 19th of May. Thereby the means of communication between Marmont's army of Portugal and Soult's of Andalusia was thrust back about a hundred miles farther up the Tagus to Toledo, (and the impediments to joint action between them seriously increased.)

It was now open to Wellington to advance either upon Salamanca, Marmont's headquarters, to north-east, or upon Madrid, Joseph's headquarters, in the east, or upon Andalusia in the south-east. He chose Salamanca because in that quarter the harvest did not ripen until August, so that Marmont would find it difficult to collect supplies. Hill was left, as usual, on the frontier between the Tagus and the Guadiana to fend off any menace in that quarter, though Soult was already tied fast to Andalusia by the considerations already mentioned, which were the more cogent since the guerilla leaders never left him a moment's peace. The French forces in the north were likewise fully occupied by Spanish troops, seconded by a British squadron on the north coast, so that little trouble was to be feared from them. But, on the other hand, Wellington was harassed by many troubles within the army. The new procedure created for regimental courts-martial had raised so rank a growth of legal technicalities that no court could see its way through them, and the enforcement of discipline had become practically impossible. In despair he wrote home for legal assistance, but meanwhile the old evils were multiplied. Next, the want of specie, always a heavy burden, had become intolerable. The pay of the troops was three months, and of the staff five months, in arrear. The Spanish muleteers, upon whom his transport depended, had not been paid for twelve months, and the outstanding bills for meat alone amounted to £200,000. To embark upon a new campaign encumbered with such pecuniary embarrassments naturally filled him with the gravest anxiety. Lastly, came a group of petty annoyances. His best intelligence officer had been taken prisoner, and there seemed no prospect of recovering him; his chief of staff had been recalled to take up a post in Ireland; and his best divisional general, Thomas Graham, and his chief commissary, Kennedy, were both obliged to go home on sick-leave. Such an accumulation of misfortunes went far to embitter the sweetness of past success.

However, on the 13th of June, Wellington crossed the Portuguese frontier with forty-three thousand men, twenty-eight thousand of them British, and fifteen thousand Portuguese; Hill being left at Merida with some twenty-two thousand men, part of them Spaniards of no great value, to watch for any French advance from Andalusia. By the 16th Wellington had reached Salamanca, Marmont, who had but two divisions, then falling back before him; and after spending a fortnight in reducing the forts of the place, which gave him seven hundred prisoners in return for five hundred casualties, he followed up Marmont to the Douro. Here there was a deadlock of a fortnight's duration until Marmont, having been reinforced, began a series of manœuvres against Wellington's line of communications, which were the easier for the Marshal since he had no such line of his own against which his opponent could retaliate. On more than one day the two armies, within a few hundred yards of each other, raced along in two parallel columns, each ready to wheel into line and attack at the slightest appearance of advantage; and it is impossible not to marvel at the nerve and skill of the two commanders who watched each other eagerly for hours in the vain search for some tactical blunder. The French always outmarched and therefore outmanœuvred the British; and Wellington having intercepted letters from Joseph announcing his intention to join Marmont with fourteen thousand men, realised that, without some unexpected stroke of good fortune, he must abandon his offensive march and retire to Portugal. Marmont, on the other hand, was so much elated with his success in manœuvre that on the 22nd of July he made a false movement which allowed his left wing to stray too far from his right. "By God, that will do," said Wellington as he saw it; and the story goes that he lay down to sleep giving orders that he should be awakened when the leading division of Marmont's left wing should have reached a certain point. Then he sprang like a lion upon the exposed wing. One of its two divisions was soon dissolved in rout, and the other crushed by a terrific cavalry attack. Marmont was wounded early, and his second in command likewise; but his successor, General Clausel, made a gallant attempt to save the day by a counter-attack. The effort failed; and then the great bulk of the French army fled in panic. The cavalry pursued, and had not a Spanish leader evacuated a certain post without orders and without informing Wellington, few of the fugitives would have escaped. The French lost fourteen thousand men, twenty guns, and two eagles. Wellington's casualties slightly exceeded five thousand. This was the Battle of Salamanca, one of the great days of the British Army. Marmont had forty-seven thousand homogeneous men with seventy-eight guns; Wellington about fifty thousand mixed British, Portuguese, and Spanish, with sixty guns; but in the actual combat seventy-four French battalions were utterly beaten by twenty-eight British and as many Portuguese battalions. Above all it was a great day for the British cavalry. "By God, Cotton," exclaimed Wellington to that General, when he returned from the charge in which he had swept everything before him. "I never saw anything so beautiful in my life; the day is *yours.*"

Clausel, after the action, retreated with all haste to Valladolid, whither Wellington followed him without great haste. The question was, what should he do next? The French were still too strong in the Peninsula for him to turn his victory to great military advantage. If he pursued

Clausel, Joseph at Madrid might advance upon his rear; if he marched upon Madrid, Clausel, after rallying his army, could descend upon his line of communications. After the event, it seems that he would have done best to ruin Clausel's army altogether and then take up a central position from which he could strike in succession at the various armies, that would certainly assemble against him, before they could join themselves together. But at the time he judged that, failing great military results from his victory, he had better content himself with moral and political advantages, and resolved to march upon Madrid. Joseph, who had returned to his capital after the news of Salamanca, evacuated it upon his approach, and after a miserable journey of hunger and thirst reached Valencia, while Wellington on the 12th of August entered Madrid amid scenes of wild enthusiasm. Clausel presently attempted the expected raid upon Wellington's communications, which brought Wellington once again to Valladolid in the first week of September; whereupon Clausel retreated to Burgos, threw a garrison of two thousand men into the castle, and fell back north-eastward to Pancorbo. Wellington thereupon advanced to Burgos, and on the 19th of September laid siege to it with three divisions, posting the remainder of the army nine miles to the north-east so as to cover the besiegers.

The siege of Burgos was the worst conducted operation in the whole of the Peninsular War. Wellington had only three heavy cannon—practically no siege-train at all,—whereas the besieged had all the reserve artillery of the army of Portugal in store; so Wellington resolved to proceed by mining. But his great fault was that he would never launch to any assault men enough to ensure success; and the result was that he sacrificed nearly two thousand men in petty attacks which were abortive, whereas if he had boldly reckoned with a thousand casualties as the cost of a single great effort, he would almost certainly have gained the castle. But, while he was thus frittering away his strength his enemies were gathering on every side. Soult, having abandoned the siege of Cadiz, was moving north to join Joseph; and only the arrival of seven thousand British from Sicily at Alicante prevented a part of the French force on the east coast from being added to them. Hill, having gathered in the British troops from Cadiz, was moving eastward up the valley of the Tagus towards Madrid; but he was too weak to withstand

[184]

Soult, and it was his intelligence of Soult's movements which caused Wellington on the 22nd of October to raise the siege of Burgos.

But he himself was also dangerously menaced from the north, for the Army of Portugal, reorganised and reinforced to a total of forty-five thousand men under General Souham, was bearing down straight upon his covering force. Unaware of Souham's strength, Wellington, though he had only twenty-one thousand British and Portuguese and twelve thousand untrustworthy Spaniards, who had lately joined him from Galicia, boldly offered him battle, which was fortunately declined. But Wellington gained a sight of the French, and, realising his danger, retreated before too late. It was everything now for him to gain time for Hill to join him, and he fell back slowly, not without sharp skirmishing, to the Douro. There he managed to hold his own until the 6th of November, when he retreated southward to the Tormes, where on the 8th Hill safely joined him. Thus Wellington, in his own phrase, "got clear in a handsome manner from the worst scrape that he ever was in."

He had now fifty-two thousand British and Portuguese and sixteen thousand Spaniards with

him, in all, sixty-eight thousand men, with one
hundred and eight guns. On the 11th of November the united French armies came up with him,
ninety thousand strong, with one hundred and
twenty guns, and with enormous superiority in
cavalry. Wellington offered them battle on his
old field of Salamanca, but Joseph would not
accept it; and on the 15th of November, Wellington
resumed his retreat upon Ciudad Rodrigo. The
army went through three miserable days. Rain
was falling in torrents, and the acting Commissary General had omitted to replenish the
magazines on the line of the retirement. There
was much indiscipline and misbehaviour among the
men; and there was one signal instance of gross
disobedience on the part of three divisional generals, who, thinking that they knew better than
Wellington, disregarded the route that he had
ordered them to follow, and found themselves
stopped by floods. Happily Soult pressed the
pursuit with little enterprise; and on the 19th the
last man of the British rearguard struggled safely
into Ciudad Rodrigo. The haven had been
reached, and the great campaign of 1812, after
many vicissitudes, was well over.

The total loss of the Allies under Wellington's

command cannot have fallen below twenty thousand men, for the retreat from Burgos of itself cost nine thousand; but, on the other hand, twenty thousand French had been made prisoners alone, to say nothing of killed and wounded; hundreds of guns had been taken in Madrid and outside Cadiz; and Spain, south of the Tagus, had been swept clear of the enemy. Moreover, the concentration of the French armies had left free play to the guerilla-bands, now more formidable than ever, and they had taken full advantage of it, so that the French operating against Wellington must have lost at least forty thousand men in all. It is true that he had been driven back to his starting-point; but at best, after his failure to take Burgos, he could hardly have expected to hold any of Spain beyond Salamanca. If he had mastered Burgos, directly on the main French line of communication with Spain, it might have served to cover his conquests; but the march to Madrid, in view of the greatly superior forces arrayed against him, was altogether too hazardous, and he paid the penalty for his mistake.

For the rest, his retreat from Burgos is regarded by foreign critics as perhaps his greatest achievement. He himself signalised its close by sending his divisional generals a circular letter, condemning in sweeping and scathing terms, without any discrimination whatever, the misconduct of the troops during their backward march. This was much resented, and justly so, for it was unfair. There had been certainly much indiscipline; but there had also been lack of food, of which Wellington seems to have been unaware. Moreover, the army had been overworked. In eleven months they had stormed two important fortresses, failed before a third, fought one great general action, besides innumerable minor engagements, and advanced, as they marched, a matter of three to four hundred miles. They were weary and stale when the time came to march back three hundred miles more, and, moreover, they were out of temper at being compelled, after so many victories, to march back at all. Wellington himself realised that they wanted rest; and it would have been better if he had made some allowance for this instead of ending the year's work by bestowing curses impartially upon all ranks. But the worst trials for himself and for his men were now nearing their end.

CHAPTER VI

WINTER-QUARTERS during the last months of 1812 and the first of 1813 were the happiest yet enjoyed by the British Army in the Peninsula. There were hunting and shooting and every kind of sport. The arrival of a trained lawyer at headquarters, with some slight amendments of legal procedure, enabled punishment to overtake evil-doers swiftly, and there was a marked improvement in discipline which reacted in a hundred ways upon the health as well as upon the behaviour of the troops. The Portuguese soldiers, thanks to Wellington's constant intercession for their regular payment and subsistence, were more efficient than they had ever been. The medical service through the exertions of Dr. Macgrigor, the principal medical officer, was admirably organised. The old Commissary General and Quartermaster-General had returned; and many inefficient generals had been sent home and replaced by able men. Moreover, there was news that Napoleon had suffered disaster in Russia, that he had lost the greater part of his four hundred thousand men, and must certainly withdraw a

[189]

number of troops from Spain. Lastly, Wellington himself had not only been created a Marquis at home, but had been accepted by the Spanish Cortes as Commander-in-Chief of the Spanish armies.

Joseph, on the other hand, was distraught by the disobedience of his subordinate generals and by the orders which he received from Napoleon to send him troops. Between him and France, too, the guerilla-leaders were active, no longer in small parties, but in military bodies four or five thousand strong, not without artillery. Practically they were masters of Biscay and Navarre; and Clausel received instructions from Paris to take four divisions and destroy them root and branch. He got to work accordingly at the end of February 1843, but had not yet accomplished his task in June, when he received an urgent summons from Joseph to break off all operations, and send every man that he could spare to Burgos.

For in the first week of May, Wellington had crossed the Portuguese frontier and waving his hand had cried, "Adieu, Portugal!" His army now numbered about one hundred thousand men, forty-seven thousand of them British, and the remainder Portuguese and Spanish; his array extending from the north-east frontier of the most

northerly province of Portugal southward to the
left bank of the Douro. The various columns
united at Toro; and Joseph, who was in inferior
strength on the Douro, retreated before them north-
eastward, past Burgos, which was evacuated without a blow, to the line of the Ebro. But he could
not stand there, for Wellington turned his northern
flank on this river as he had turned it on the line of
the Douro, and he was fain to retire to Vitoria.
There, with fifty thousand men, he halted in the
basin that lies to south of the town and decided to
fight what may be called a delaying action in order
to cover his further retreat, for Clausel with his four
divisions, though long since summoned, had not yet
reached him. Wellington, with seventy-two thousand sabres and bayonets, therefore greatly outnumbered him; and, if his plans had been executed
aright, the battle of the 21st of June would have
made an end of Joseph's army. As things fell
out, the whole of the French artillery—one hundred
and fifty pieces—and their baggage, down even to
the officers' love-letters, were captured; but the
army escaped with the loss of about seven thousand
killed, wounded and taken, Wellington's casualties
amounting to about five thousand, of which nearly
four-fifths were British.

[191]

The pursuit was not at the outset well pressed, for once again the discipline of the British had failed with victory. The men had had a great opportunity for plunder, and some had appropriated so much money that they became careful of their lives, while others had so gorged themselves with food and drink that they could hardly move. However, Joseph's defeated army was driven across the Pyrenees, and Wellington, on reaching Pamplona, decided to hunt him no farther. Clausel, meanwhile, took his troops to Zaragoza, whence he could join either Joseph or General Suchet, who remained on the east coast, the more secure since General John Murray, who commanded the British troops in that quarter, had as usual conducted his operations with miserable feebleness and inefficiency. Clausel, however, soon found himself in hopeless difficulties owing to the activity of the guerilla-bands, and on the 13th of July, eluding Wellington's efforts to intercept him, he joined Joseph on the northern slopes of the Western Pyrenees.

It was essential, before Wellington could continue his advance, to master the fortresses of San Sebastian and Pamplona. The latter was blockaded; and the siege of San Sebastian, which was quite a little place with a garrison of three thousand men, was entrusted to Sir Thomas Graham, with one British division and one Portuguese brigade. The operations were mismanaged. After a fortnight's cannonade an assault was delivered on the 25th of July and was beaten back with the loss of four hundred men. The siege was then turned for a time into a blockade owing to want of ammunition; and meanwhile Napoleon, upon hearing the news of Vitoria, sent Soult back to take command of all the troops that were or till lately had been in Spain. Upon his arrival on the 13th of July Joseph sneaked away, and Jourdan, his late chief of staff, who was in no way responsible for Joseph's misfortunes, was relegated by Napoleon's order to an obscure house in the provinces.

Soult was a coarse, avaricious, surly man, whose Army of Andalusia had been the most rapacious, the most disorderly, the most encumbered with women, and the worst disciplined of all the French forces in Spain; but he was none the less a very able administrator and possessed remarkable strategic gifts, failing only, through weakness and irresolution, on the actual field of battle. Having made up his army to about seventy thousand men, and restored, more or less, their discipline and organization, he, on the 20th of July, essayed a great counter-attack along the three main valleys of the Pyrenees which lead to Pamplona, hoping to raise the blockade both of that place and of San Sebastian, and even to drive the British back to the Ebro. In so difficult a country Wellington could not be everywhere; and his divisional generals, lions (as he phrased it) when under his eye, but children when they were not, or the most part lost their heads and gave way. One of them was so much interested in the action of the division nearest to him that he forgot to look after his own, which, like the others, was forced back for some distance. He described this as the result of an unfortunate accident. "Yes," retorted Wellington with biting sarcasm, "the unfortunate accident that you were absent when the attack was made." However, Soult's plans went by no means as he had intended; and it was more by accident than by design that on the 26th of July he found himself at Sorauren confronting sixteen thousand of Wellington's men with thirty thousand of his own. He was hesitating whether to attack or not when Wellington galloped up to the top of the hill over against him amid a roar of cheering from his own men. A very deep valley separated the two commanders, who stood only five hundred yards apart,[1] and Soult, hesitating, decided to put off his attack until the morrow, giving time for more British troops to come up. None the less it was with no more than the sixteen thousand that Wellington beat the thirty thousand the next day, when the French crossed the deep valley and climbed the desperately steep hill in a gallant but ineffectual attempt to drive the British from it. The old defect of the French armies told. The troops were not fed, and the half-starved men were too weak and exhausted to stand the strain. They were repulsed with great slaughter, and then Wellington, having assembled his troops, took the offensive in his turn and drove the French back, after six more days of fighting, as a mere demoralised mob to their former position. Wellington always said and believed that if three British marauders had not been captured by the French and given warning of the proximity of the British troops, Soult and his whole army would have been captured; but in the light of certain facts this is impossible. The Marshal, however, admitted a loss of thirteen thousand men, whereas Wellington's casualties little exceeded seven thousand.

[1] The conformation of the ground is such that one can fix the places where the two generals stood with absolute certainty.

Wellington then turned his thoughts to San Sebastian, where the siege was now resumed, and on the 31st of August the place was taken by storm. Once again the troops engaged, to Wellington's fury, took leave of all discipline, being very savage; and the excesses at San Sebastian were even worse than at Badajoz. On that very day Soult made his last effort to rescue the doomed fortress by another general attack on the allied army, but was beaten off after two days' fighting, with a loss of nearly four thousand men. Thereupon Wellington decided to take the offensive in his turn and to attack the fortified lines which Soult had thrown up south of the river Bidassoa for defence of the French frontier. These were carried with little difficulty on the 7th of October, Soult's dispositions being vicious and his handling of his troops thoroughly bad; and the Marshal fell back to another position a short distance to northward and began to fortify that. His troops were by this time thoroughly demoralised by defeat; but he did at least his best to keep them together.

Wellington, for his part, was unwilling for the present to advance farther. Pamplona was still untaken in his rear; and Napoleon, having raised

another great army, was boldly facing the hosts of
the Allies in Germany. Wellington had no great
opinion of the plans of the Austrians and Prussians
in that quarter, and it was always possible that the
Emperor might inflict on them some great defeat, scare them into accepting terms, as his way
was, and then turn all his strength upon the frontier of Spain. Wellington's last movement had
brought his troops on to high ground, where they
suffered so much from rain and snow that he longed
to bring them forward, but not until Pamplona fell
on the 25th of October could he venture to move.
Meanwhile his troubles were many. The Spanish
and Portuguese Governments, now that they were
safe and delivered from the enemy, both turned
against him. During his advance from Spain he
had shifted his maritime base from Lisbon first to
St Ander and later to the little port of Passages;
but the British Navy seemed unable to keep his
communications by sea secure. Lastly, the terms
of many soldiers, who had been enlisted for short
service, had expired, which gave much trouble,
until the Government decided to give them a
bounty to re-enlist. It seemed as though one set
of difficulties had been overcome only to raise many

even more thorny and embarrassing. But this, after all, is what generally happens in war.

At last, set free by the fall of Pamplona, Wellington on the 10th of November attacked Soult's fortified position on the river Nivelle. The enterprise was successful so far as it went, for the entrenchments, though of great strength, were easily carried, and sixty-nine guns were captured; but Wellington had counted upon cutting off the retreat of a large body of French troops; and this operation miscarried. However, he was at last fairly established on the plains of France; and now came the moment of real anxiety. The tone and conduct of the Spanish Government showed Wellington clearly that, if he should suffer defeat, retreat into Spain would be impossible. All now depended upon the behaviour of his troops. If they conducted themselves well towards the French inhabitants and treated them with kindness and forbearance, paying for all they took, all would go smoothly. The population would even welcome the British Army to save them from their own, whose only idea of subsistence was to live upon the country which they occupied and pay for nothing. It was soon proved that the British Army had at last learned the lesson which Wellington for years had tried so hard to teach. Not only did the men conduct themselves very well, but there appeared "a new spirit among the officers" to keep them in strict order. The Spaniards, on the other hand, could not be brought to abstain from retaliation for all the sufferings that they had endured; and Wellington took the extreme step of sending most of them back into their own country. "With forty thousand Spaniards I don't know where I should stop," he wrote at this time, "but, if they plunder, they will ruin all." Never was there a general who, not less from humanity than from policy, was more resolute against oppression of the peaceful population in war.

On the 8th of December came the great news of the overthrow of Napoleon by the allied nations at Leipzig, with orders from the British Government to prosecute the invasion of France. Soult, after being thrown back from Nivelle, had taken up a position to south of Bayonne, throwing up an entrenched camp of great strength on both banks of the river Nive; and here Wellington attacked him on the 9th of December, repelling sharp counter-attacks on the two following days. The operations were delicate and difficult, because the rivers were liable to sudden floods which defied all calculations; and so it was that, owing to the washing away of a bridge, General Hill found himself on the morning of the 13th totally isolated with a force of no more than fourteen thousand men and fourteen guns. Soult seized the opportunity to attack him with more than twenty thousand men and thirty guns. The fight, called by the name of St Pierre, lasted from daylight until sunset and was extraordinarily bloody, the French losing three thousand and the British and Allies sixteen to seventeen hundred; but Hill's victory was complete, and, as Wellington joyfully told him, was all his own.

Meanwhile the coalised Powers of Europe, after their great victory at Leipzig, had fallen at variance among themselves, and had finally devised a plan for the invasion of France which Wellington promptly and rightly condemned as hopelessly bad. Napoleon too was negotiating for peaceable withdrawal of his few remaining troops from the east coast of Spain; and there was good prospect that, after striking one or two telling blows against the armies of the coalition, he would turn upon Wellington in overwhelming strength and compel

him to embark for England. Wellington therefore decided that it would be imprudent to under-
take any further enterprise than the investment
of Bayonne; but to do this it was necessary to
cross the broad and deep river Adour and manœuvre Soult out of his position upon it. After
much delay through bad weather this was effected
by a series of skilful movements between the
17th and 24th of February 1814; and Soult being
thus, so to speak, forced into the open, marched
eastward with thirty-seven thousand men to Orthez.
On the 26th Wellington crossed the Adour by a
bridge laid on twenty-six coasting craft—one of
the masterpieces of the officers of the Staff Corps,
—and, leaving a sufficient force to contain the
garrison left by Soult in Bayonne, followed up the
Marshal with thirty-three thousand men, and
overtook him in a strong position to north of
Orthez. Though inferior in numbers he attacked
him on the 27th, and for a time the British made
no great progress. But the issue of the action
was never for a moment in real doubt. Napier
tells a story that Soult, believing that for once he
was to be victorious, slapped his thigh and cried,
"At last I have him!" but careful survey of the
fight proves this to be without foundation. The

French were driven off with the loss of four thousand killed, wounded, and prisoners. Wellington's causalties fell just below two thousand; and, had he not himself been disabled by a contusion from a bullet which prevented him from sitting in the saddle, the pursuit would have been more closely pressed, and the French would have suffered more severely.

Soult retreated eastward, Wellington following him up closely; but heavy rain within the next few days brought both armies to a standstill, and contact between them was lost. In a country which is one network of rapid rivers flowing down from the snows of the Pyrenees, temporary and pontoon bridges were quickly swept away by floods, and Soult was careful to destroy the permanent bridges behind him. Wellington took the opportunity to occupy Bordeaux as his new base on the sea; and on the 13th of March Soult moved up to his outposts as if to attack, but thought better of it and fell back slowly southward. He had Napoleon's orders to keep the field of action as close as possible to the Pyrenees, and tried thus to execute them. Very critical events had passed during this time. The armies of the coalised Powers in their invasion of France had unduly dispersed their forces; and Napoleon on the 10th of February had opened a masterly campaign, striking heavy blows right and left, until by the middle of March the Powers, in fear and trembling, decided to concentrate to the rear. Had he continued the same system with patience for a little longer, it was Wellington's mature opinion that he would have prevented the allied armies from reaching Paris; and it was therefore not without apprehension that on the 18th of March with an army now raised, chiefly by a contingent of Spaniards, to fifty thousand men, he resumed his pursuit of Soult.

The Marshal had not shone in his operations since his first defeat in the Pyrenees, and he did not improve now. On the 20th he fought a useless little action at Tarbes, which only delayed his retreat to no purpose and compelled him to take the longer of two roads to his next point, Toulouse. Wellington thereupon followed the shorter road; and Soult, in order to arrive there before him, was compelled to hustle his wretched troops on at a speed which put an end to all order and discipline. Nevertheless, Wellington advanced slowly and with the greatest caution. Not only was the rain incessant, but he had no late news of the situation in Europe; and a report had reached him that Napoleon had fallen back to Orléans, which might mean that he intended to join Soult, and raise all southern France against his enemies. Not until the 26th did Wellington come up before Toulouse; and on the previous day, though of course he knew it not, all his anxieties had been brought to an end by Napoleon himself. The Emperor had sacrificed the fruits of his marvellous campaign by marching eastward against the rear and communication of the Allies and leaving open to them the road to Paris. After some hesitation they decided to take the chance thus given to them; and from that moment the fall of Napoleon was certain.

Ignorant, of course, of all this, Wellington proceeded with the work in hand. Soult's position at Toulouse was very strong, and the preliminary operations, before it was possible even to approach him, were very delicate. Wellington, however, who had thoroughly learned his opponent's ways and weaknesses, took every imaginable liberty and did so with impunity. Finally, on the 10th of April, he closed with his enemy, and then took the greatest liberties of all. He actually made a flank march of two miles across the front of the French position and within cannon-shot of it, before wheeling his troops into line and hurling them at what were, practically, the outworks of a fortress. From so dangerous a manœuvre success was hardly to be expected, except as part of a perfectly combined attack at other points; and it so happened that owing to the misfortunes of some of his subordinate leaders, and the bungling of others, the whole of his plans miscarried. His losses amounted to over four thousand, whereas Soult's did not exceed half as many; and in fact John Colborne, the future Lord Seaton, roundly declared that both the plan and the execution of the battle were as faulty as they could be. Even the French, when the war was over, were inclined to claim it as a success, and Marshal Suchet asked Wellington's leave to submit to him a plan of the action so that the exact positions of the regiments engaged might be clearly marked thereon. The plan was duly laid before him, and was found to be covered with such remarks as: "At this point twelve British battalions were overthrown," "Here the General smashed a British regiment," and so forth. "What a beautiful plan!" said Wellington gravely, "and so perfectly drawn! really it is wonderfully done. Pray return it to Marshal Suchet with my compliments and thanks." Nothing more was heard of the plan after this. Toulouse was certainly not one of Wellington's happiest efforts; but at the moment Soult knew well that he was beaten, and showed it by evacuating the city on the 12th and resuming his retreat.

On that day news reached Wellington of the fall of Napoleon and of the establishment of a provisional government at Paris. He duly forwarded the despatch to Soult, but, through no fault of the Marshal's, the garrison of Bayonne made a sortie which brought on a sharp engagement on the 14th. By the 18th all had been adjusted; an agreement for a suspension of arms was signed, and the Peninsular War was over.

English historians have by tacit accord conspired to dwell upon Wellington's last operations in the Pyrenees and in France at much less length than on his earlier exploits in Portugal and Spain; and in this work I must confess that I have been a party to the conspiracy. One reason is the intricacy of the country owing to mountains on both sides of the Franco-Spanish marches, and to rivers on the French territory immediately to north of the frontier. There are comparatively recent maps of all French ground, but they are all upon a small scale and by no means remarkable for accuracy. On the Spanish side there are large tracts which have never been surveyed at all, and of which the best maps that exist—and they are very imperfect—are those drawn up by the Quartermaster-General's Department of Wellington's army. Language is another stumbling-block in examining this sphere of operations, for Basque is a prohibitive tongue to all but those who are born to speak it, and hence inquiry is difficult and answers unintelligible.

But perhaps the principal cause of this comparative indifference to the story of the war in France is that the French army never recovered its *morale* after Vitoria, and that Wellington's task thereby became so much the easier. It is a singular fact that the private narratives of officers and soldiers who fought under Wellington, though they go deeply into detail over the earlier campaigns, pass comparatively lightly over the work done in France, and hardly trouble themselves with the fighting in the Pyrenees. Indeed the historian was until quite lately driven back upon Napier, whose violent prejudice in Soult's favour vitiates not only his judgment but his actual statement of events, and upon Wellington's own public despatches, which, like all other public despatches, leave a great many things unsaid. It is only within the last ten years that a French officer, gathering his material from original matter in the French archives, as well as from every printed book, English or French, that he could lay his hands on, has at last made the course of the operations following upon the Battle of Vitoria comparatively clear. Writing with admirable accuracy and impartiality he shows, in particular, how the British army worked as one, whereas the French was torn by internal dissensions and by insubordination. Wellington, as we have seen, did not spare hard criticism of his divisional commanders, but it is very clear that they knew their business much better, and were far more loyal in labouring for the common welfare and success, than their rivals upon the French side. It is possible to argue that Soult was ungenial and unpopular, and that the French generals would have wrought with greater intelligence and a better will under some greater chief, or some stricter disciplinarian such as Davoust. But it is to be remarked that Massena, a far abler soldier than Soult, who by sheer tenacity of purpose kept his starving army before the lines of

Torres Vedras for weeks, failed equally to obtain loyalty and cordial co-operation from his subordinates. Under Napoleon himself things would doubtless have been better; yet I doubt greatly whether, even under his command, the French army would have acted with the same singleness of purpose as the British and Portuguese under Wellington's. The truth is that the real spirit of discipline never was in Napoleon's armies, and that it could not be, because they lived chiefly by marauding.

It was this—one cannot too often repeat it,—that Wellington from the first recognised; and it may be said that throughout his time in the Peninsula he was training his army for the invasion of France. We have seen something of his difficulties and of their source, and have been eye-witnesses of his deep disgust when at every fresh trial, from the retreat from Talavera to the storm of San Sebastian, the men fell back into their old evil ways. Englishmen drank hard in those days, and the wine-vaults of Spain were a terrible temptation. Harry Smith has drawn for us a ludicrous picture of the Light Division essaying to make a night-march, when every soul, except himself, was drunk; the commanding general in particular being so much exhilarated by wine that no entreaties

French inhabitants. Well had Wellington verified his prediction that when once the seat of war were transferred to French soil, hostilities would speedily end.

His great triumph came when the regiments sailed away either for service in America or for return to England. One division traversed the greater part of France to its port of embarkation not only without a single crime, but without a single complaint of any inhabitant against a single British soldier. Wellington in the past few months had been created a Knight of the Garter as well as a Marquis, but these honours must have seemed to him very paltry in comparison with the tribute paid to him by his own soldiers through their emulation of his example in dealing gently and mercifully with their fallen enemies.

CHAPTER VII

THE cessation of hostilities brought no rest to Wellington. He was promoted to a dukedom on the 11th of May; but there was no question of allowing him to rest on his laurels, for his advice and his service were sought for by the Government in all difficulties. Castlereagh at once offered him the post of Ambassador at Paris; and, though he had not been in England since 1809, he promptly signified his readiness to stay abroad for any time that his duty to the public might require. But first he went on a diplomatic mission in May to Madrid, where he was well received but was doubtful of his success, and returning to France early in June made at last for London which he reached on the 23rd. Parliament had already made him a grant of four hundred thousand pounds; and he now received further the thanks of both Houses. His face was still unknown to the public, and he continued to be no more than a great name. The caricaturists, knowing nothing of his features, had portrayed him as a bull-dog, pinning Napoleon by the throat, with the name "Wellington" written on the collar to establish his identity.

[213]

By the middle of August he was abroad again,
first to inspect and report upon the frontier of the
Netherlands—a journey on which he took note of
the position of Waterloo—and at the end of the
month to take up his duties in Paris. Before he
had been there six months he was sent to fill the
place of Castlereagh at the Congress of Vienna,
where on the 7th of March he received the news of
Napoleon's escape from Elba. He recommended
the British Government to throw its army at once
into the Netherlands, and lingered at Vienna only
to set his hand to a new treaty of the allied Powers,
and to their public manifesto declaring Napoleon to
be an outlaw. It is characteristic of the malignity
of the Whigs against him that, in consequence of
this latter act, he was denounced in the House of
Commons as abetting an openly expressed intention to assassinate Bonaparte. The Opposition
could never forgive him the victories which had for
so long maintained the Tories in office.

Arriving on the 29th of March at Brussels he was
dismayed at the nature of the British force which
was to be placed under his command. Ministers
could not immediately send him more than six
regiments of cavalry and twenty-five battalions of
infantry; and of those twenty-five, fifteen were

[214]

confessedly "weak and inefficient corps" which had been scraped together for Sir Thomas Graham's raid upon the Low Countries in 1814, and had been kept there ever since. Of the remaining ten, six had served in the Peninsula, but had lost many veteran soldiers through expiration of their term of service, while two more were composed of boys, half-trained and unfit for serious work. As to the rest of the Peninsular army, many regiments had been sent across to America for the war in that quarter, and had not yet had time to return, while others had been hastily disbanded. Moreover, owing to certain legal difficulties, it was impossible to call out the Militia in order to liberate all regular troops for foreign service; and this defect was only remedied by the passing of two Acts on the 14th of June, four days before the Battle of Waterloo, and therefore just a little late.

With cavalry the Government could be more liberal, there being little demand for that arm in America; and the six regiments ready for immediate service had all served in the Peninsula; but they were very weak and could only put three squadrons apiece, instead of four, into the field. The artillery was in the worst state of all. There was plenty of guns and of ammunition, but owing

to imprudent discharges of men, there were few
gunners and still fewer drivers. Wellington asked
for one hundred and fifty cannon, but the Master-
General of the Ordnance could not immediately
supply gunners for more than forty-two, nor did he
see his way to providing drivers except by enlisting
unemployed postboys for short terms, and offering
bounties to such Hanoverians as might be ready
to accept four guineas. Peace had been signed on
the 30th of May 1814, and by the first week of
March 1815 England had been reduced by the
clamour of Parliament to sheer military impotence.

Over and above the British troops, there was the
King's German Legion, some part of which had
fortunately been halted in the Netherlands while
on their way to Hanover for disbandment. Most
of these had served under Wellington in the
Peninsula and were excellent troops, though the
infantry was weak in numbers. There was also the
Hanoverian militia, twenty-five battalions strong,
with a few cavalry and artillery. These were good
material, but only half-trained and very short of
officers. Wellington wished to transfer as many
of the militia as possible to the infantry of the
Legion, whose veterans would keep them steady;
but, in the face of his entreaties, the Hanoverian

Government insisted on robbing the Legion of veteran officers and sergeants to make good the deficiencies of the militia. There is something almost comical in this arrogant rejection by civilians of advice from the one general who had always beaten the French.

There remained the allied troops who were to serve under Wellington's command. First of these were the Dutch, about whom there were contradictory reports. Their spirit was said to be good, but many of the officers and men had been in the service of Napoleon, and felt the bond of comradeship with the French army. Moreover, their Minister of War was a general who had fought unsuccessfully against the British both at the Cape and in Java, and could not be expected to feel very friendly towards them, while the officers in charge of every department under him were cordially in favour of France. The Commander-in-Chief was the Prince of Orange, who had been on Wellington's staff in more than one Peninsular campaign. He was a soldier of small capacity but great ambition, who had only with difficulty been restrained from advancing and fighting Napoleon single-handed when he arrived in France from Elba. His Quartermaster-General, Major-General Constant de Rebecque, who had served with him in the Peninsular, was loyal, able, and energetic. His royal father, the King of the Netherlands, steadily obstructed all of Wellington's proposals until the Duke declined to have anything more to do with him, when His Majesty gracefully gave way, and made over to him the supreme command of all his troops, with the rank of Field-Marshal.

The Belgians were more doubtful even than the Dutch, and, to speak plainly, were bad and untrustworthy troops. They had some excuse, for they too had links of comradeship with the French army, and, moreover, Belgium had, by no will of its own, been annexed to Holland, so that all soldiers had been enlisted in the service of the King of the Netherlands, whom they detested. Wellington expected little of them, and he was not disappointed. He was anxious to import ten thousand of the Portuguese veterans who had fought well for him in the Peninsula; but the proposal found no favour at Lisbon, and was abandoned as impracticable.

Altogether the Duke was justified in describing his army as infamous. Inferior though most of his British troops were, they were still the best that he had, and he expended endless ingenuity in so intermingling the component parts of his heterogenous host that there should be some element of stability in every division of his hundred thousand men. Most of his divisional and brigade commanders were old Peninsular men, but his tried chief of staff, George Murray, had been sent to Canada, and Wellington had to content himself with one of Murray's former deputies. Kennedy also was not with him; but his Chief Commissary was at least a man of experience whom Graham had summoned from the Peninsular army in 1814. He had, however, his famous officer, Colquhoun Grant, to take charge of the intelligence. Nevertheless Wellington found himself in 1815 in much the same position as when he landed in Portugal in 1809. He had troops, but they needed to be made into an army, and there was now very little time wherein to accomplish the task.

Of the Allies that were to act immediately with him, the Prussians were set down as one hundred and twenty thousand men. The quality of these left much to be desired. Nearly half of the infantry was mere militia, and the rest included many raw recruits and men enlisted in provinces only recently acquired by Prussia. Their clothing, equipment, and armament were very defective, there being in some regiments as many as three different calibres of musket. The cavalry was in even worse condition than the infantry. The artillery was well provided with guns, but, as with the British, short of trained gunners. The Commander-in-Chief, Blücher, though rough and illiterate, was a fine fighting soldier and despite of his seventy-one years, both active and energetic. The chief of his staff, Gneisenau, was supposed to make good Blücher's intellectual defects, having a great reputation as a strategist. He was, however, a poor commander in the field and an indifferent tactician; and was, further, conceited, jealous, and suspicious. None the less, his talents, backed by the character of Blücher, who trusted him implicitly, made a strong combination.

In the general plan of campaign Wellington's army was supposed to form the extreme right of a host of some six hundred thousand British, Germans, Austrians, and Russians, who were to invade France from the north and east; but at the end of May only the troops of Blücher and Wellington, above named, were in place; and the date when the rest might be expected was extremely uncertain. The space assigned for Wellington's advance was between Maubeuge and Beaumont, and for

Blücher's, immediately on his left, between Philippeville and Givet.

Napoleon on his side hoped to put half a million men into the field by August, but meanwhile he could count only upon some two hundred thousand, of which, after making provisions for other points of danger, he purposed to lead about one hundred and twenty-four thousand under his personal command to the north. This force he distributed into five corps under d'Erlon, Reille, Vandamme, Gérard, and Lobau, of whom the first two had suffered many a buffet from Wellington in France and Spain. Grouchy was in charge of the cavalry, and Drouot of the Imperial Guard; and for chief of staff, since Berthier could not return to him, he selected Soult. Though, therefore, Napoleon had not met the British himself since the siege of Toulon in 1793, he had plenty of men about him who knew the red-coats in action.

As regards plans, the Emperor built all his hopes upon an early success in Belgium. The newly established King of the Netherlands had just set up his capital at Brussels. The restored King of France, Louis XVIII, had taken refuge at Ghent. If he could expel both of these potentates ignominiously by a great victory and a triumphant progress through the Belgic provinces, he might revive the old legend of his invincibility, rally the Dutch and Belgians once again to his standards, and—greatest object of all—bring about the fall of the British Ministry which had for so long contended against him. The advent of a new British Cabinet would mean the reversal of their predecessors' policy; and the withdrawal of England from the coalition would signify the dissolution of the coalition's armies, which, without British subsidies, would be unable to keep the field. The game, though hazardous, was a bold one; but war is always a gamble, and of all men who have made war, Napoleon, who invariably staked double or quits, was the hardiest and most desperate gambler.

Wellington was fully aware of Napoleon's hopes and realised that upon him in 1815, as through all the weary years since 1809, depended the life of the Ministry, and the ultimate issue of the long war against revolutionary and Imperial France. Upon him also were thrown a thousand matters derived from the past in Spain and Portugal, concerning the present in keeping the coalition together and arranging for the subsistence of his own and Blücher's armies in the Netherlands, and concerning the future government that was to be established in France. As to military operations, he desired above all, if possible, to keep the war within the borders of France, judging that the inhabitants would soon weary of a French army that lived upon them; though it was by no means certain that the Dutch and Prussians would behave as well towards the people in the north of France as the British had conducted themselves in the south. There was, however, a technical difficulty in the way, the same that had hampered the British Government in the matter of calling out the Militia. It was by no means certain whether a state of hostilities existed between any two countries in Europe. England and the Allies were not at war with France, but with the revolted soldiery which had restored Napoleon, and, until the whereabouts of that soldiery should be known, it was impossible to move troops against them. And this was a very great embarrassment. "In the situation in which we are placed at present," wrote Wellington on the 11th of May, "neither at war nor at peace, unable on that account to patrol up to the enemy and ascertain his position by view, or to act offensively upon any part of his line, it is difficult, if not impossible, to combine our operations because there are no data upon which to found a combination." Such a situation suited Napoleon exactly, and he upheld the fiction of no state of war as ardently as anyone. The British fleet, less squeamish than its brethren ashore, had begun to take prizes as early as in March; but as late as on the 7th of June Napoleon denounced the capture of a French frigate in the Mediterranean as "bloodshed during peace." These peculiar conditions had not a little effect on the course of the subsequent military operations.

In these circumstances, Wellington could only canton his troops across the route whereby he expected Napoleon to advance—between the Scheldt and the Sambre—and, since the line of the Prussian communications ran eastward and that of the British westward, he came to an agreement with Blücher that, if Napoleon should try to drive a wedge between the two armies, the British should sacrifice their line and throw themselves upon that of the Prussians. Meanwhile Napoleon continued to conceal his own preparations behind the screen of fortresses and forests on the French frontier; and, concerting his movements with admirable skill, he crossed the Sambre at Charleroi and Marchienne on the morning of the 15th of June, and drove back the Prussian covering troops with the loss of some twelve hundred killed, wounded, and prisoners.

By nightfall he had one hundred and twenty thousand men compactly bivouacked within the quadrilateral Frasnes, Fleurus, Châtelet, Marchienne, on a front of about four miles and a depth of about six. The foremost troops lay within less than twenty-five miles of Brussels, and his advanced cavalry had penetrated as far as Quatre Bras on the road to that city, before it had been checked and had fallen back to Frasnes. The Emperor had won the first point in the game. With his army organised into two wings and a reserve, he had struck at the point of junction between Wellington and Blücher. The Prussians, after their brush with him north of the Sambre, had fallen back eastward. The troops encountered on the road to Brussels had been ascertained to belong to Wellington's army. To all appearance he had driven a wedge between the British and Prussians, and could deal with them in detail in accordance with his plans.

There can be no question but that the Allies were taken completely by surprise. Wellington's troops were dispersed along a line extending from

Brussels westward for fully forty miles, while Blücher's were stretched over a still wider area to the east, and had hardly begun their concentration. How this came about never has been and never will be explained. The impossibility of patrolling up to the French army was no doubt one cause; and the Prussians were something more than slow in informing Wellington of their first contact with the French troops. But it seems certain that, through some accident, one of Wellington's most trusted intelligencers failed him. The fact is curious, for the British always contrive by some means to penetrate their enemies' secrets. Colquhoun Grant was not a man to be easily baffled; and the fact that the ordinary military means of obtaining information were closed to Wellington must have prompted him to urge special vigilance upon his intelligence department. It should seem, however, that both Wellington and Blücher were so confident, owing to their numerical superiority, that they did somewhat neglect ordinary military precautions. The ultimate result justified their confidence; but the immediate result was to give them three very anxious days.

There was nothing for the allied commanders to do but to effect their concentration as rapidly as possible. But the difficulty for Wellington was to know where to concentrate. The Prussians had told him nothing, not even that Charleroi was in the hands of the French; and he had no signs to show him whether the French were likely to advance upon Brussels from Charleroi, or whether he should await them further westward by way of Mons. Not until ten o'clock on the night of the 15th did he at last hear from Mons that there was no alarm on that side, whereupon he issued orders for his army to make a general movement eastward, and for Picton's division, which lay at Brussels, to march southward about eight miles to Mont St Jean, on the road to Quatre Bras. Fortunately, the Dutch general Constant de Rebecque took it upon himself to order two Dutch brigades, of his own motion, to Quatre Bras, a place of vital importance to the junction of the British and Prussian armies.

The Duchess of Richmond was giving a ball in Brussels that night, and thither Wellington repaired with ostentatious lightness of heart. Towards one o'clock in the morning he there received a message from Constant de Rebecque that the French cavalry had penetrated as far as Quatre Bras on the previous day, and that he had increased the strength of the troops there, and had warned others to be ready to proceed thither. Wellington coolly called his superior officers together, explained the situation to them, and bade them slip away from the ball quietly and repair to their posts with all speed. At two o'clock he withdrew himself and went to bed, to be awakened two or three hours later by another messenger from Mons. He sent him on to Picton with orders for that general to take his division at once forward to Quatre Bras; and shortly afterwards he decided definitely that that village must be his point of concentration. Whether the French advance along that road were a feint or not, he must be at hand to support the Prussians in case they should be attacked. Finally, an hour or so later he started for Quatre Bras.

Reaching the village at nine o'clock, he found some Prussian stragglers, from whom at last he obtained some information of what had happened on the previous day. He was surprised and almost incredulous, as well he might be, considering the neglect of the Prussian staff. He warmly commended Constant for the measures that he had taken for the protection of Quatre Bras, on his own responsibility and even overruling Welling-

ton's own orders. There were as yet only six thousand five hundred infantry and eight guns, with no
cavalry, on the spot; but more would be coming up
every hour, and so far there was no sign of any
movement on the part of the enemy. At half-past
ten, having at length discovered where Blücher
was to be found, he wrote him a letter describing
the position of his troops as his staff represented
it to him to be. The description was altogether
inaccurate; and German writers have insinuated
that it was given in order to deceive Blücher and
make him fight a battle to cover the concentration
of the Anglo-Netherlandish army. Wellington,
however, gave it in all good faith, and based his
own actions upon it. Moreover, Blücher had
already decided to fight; and Wellington riding
over to Ligny shortly afterwards to meet him,
found him drawing up his army for battle. The
Prussian dispositions were radically vicious; and
Wellington ventured to hint that, if his own troops
were so drawn up, he should expect them to be
beaten. But Gneisenau was not the man to listen
to advice, and only begged that Wellington would
bring up as large a portion of his force as possible
to act as reserve to the Prussian army. The Duke
had his doubts whether this would be the most

profitable method of employing his troops, but said at last, "Well, I will come if I am not attacked myself," and so rode back to Quatre Bras.

Napoleon, meanwhile, had only very vague knowledge of the doings of the Allies, and seems to have suffered from considerable confusion of thought as to his own intentions. He had made up his mind that Wellington and Blücher had retreated in different directions, and at the outset he expected no fighting at all on the 16th. He gave Ney, who commanded his left wing, to understand that he would meet with little opposition at Quatre Bras, and planned to meet him there in the evening and march with him to Brussels. Later, finding that Blücher had concentrated a considerable force at Ligny, he bade Ney make an end of the enemy at Quatre Bras as speedily as possible, and then join him in overwhelming the Prussians. The result of the first message was that Ney did not hurry himself, and that his foremost troops did not come up to Quatre Bras until two in the afternoon. By that time the allied troops on the spot numbered seven thousand, with sixteen guns. Ney had under his hand or within easy call forty-two thousand men and ninety-two guns, but he opened his attack with no more than eight thousand and six guns.

WELLINGTON

In order to make a show of strength the allied troops had been aligned along a front of two miles. Most of the Netherlandish regiments made but a poor resistance, and the French were carrying everything before them, when Picton's division began to come up. In order to gain time, Wellington launched the foremost of them to a counter-attack, which secured respite sufficient for drawing up the rest of the division and for the arrival of further driblets of reinforcements. Ney thereupon assailed Wellington's position in strength, but without success; and then came an urgent message from Soult repeating Napoleon's order that he should make an end of the enemy at Quatre Bras and hasten to complete the overthrow of the Prussians at Ligny. Ney lost his temper. One corps, twenty thousand strong, under d'Erlon, had already been withdrawn from him; and he decided that he would trample down all opposition by a great onslaught of cavalry. But this also failed for, though punished heavily by Ney's artillery in the intervals between the charges, the British infantry in squares would not be broken. There were many critical moments during the day, but always Wellington was at hand to tide them over. At one moment he had to gallop for his

life and jump a ditch full of Highlanders in order
to escape from the French cavalry; but wherever
the danger was greatest he was to be found, calm
and collected, directing the fight. As the hours
passed, more and more of the Allies, British and
foreign, came up until their numbers became
superior to Ney's; and at nightfall the Marshal
fell back, repulsed, to Frasnes. He had lost about
forty-two hundred men, and the Allies rather
more, for many of the Netherlanders had vanished
unhurt from the field.

Meanwhile Blücher had been beaten at Ligny.
He had eighty-two thousand men against Napoleon's sixty-five thousand, and should at least
have made a drawn battle, if not a victory, of the
encounter; but defeated he was, though far from
decisively, and only after a very stubborn fight.
The gallant old man had been unhorsed when leading a charge of cavalry, and had been ridden over,
trampled on, and much shaken physically, but his
spirit was quite unbroken and his fighting energy
unabated. About ten thousand of his army were
reduced to a rabble, but the greater part retreated
in good order. Gneisenau was for falling back
eastward on Liège, leaving Wellington to shift
for himself; but Blücher prevailed on him to change

the direction from eastward to northward, and to name Wavre, about thirteen miles south-east of Brussels, as the place. There was one corps, Bülow's, forty thousand strong, which had not had time to reach Ligny, and another which had been little engaged; and these would suffice to hearten the remainder of the army, itself not greatly discouraged, to a fresh effort. One thing, however, the Prussian staff omitted to do, namely, to inform Wellington of the result of the battle and of their movements in consequence.

Though it might not be obvious to Wellington and Blücher, the 16th of June had been a bad day for Napoleon. It was no part of his principles or plans that both of his wings should be heavily engaged on the same day. His design was to turn the bulk of his strength upon one opponent only, using one wing, with possibly part of the other, and his reserve for the purpose; but he had found himself saddled simultaneously with two pitched battles, one for each wing, and, to make the issue decisive, the reserve was needed by both. He and Ney both clamoured for this reserve, and the result had been that d'Erlon's corps had spent the day walking backwards and forwards between Quatre Bras and Ligny, and had taken no share in either

engagement. As Wellington said later, if he and
not Napoleon had so mishandled his troops, his
reputation as a general would have gone for ever.
There, however, the matter was, and the Emperor
in the early hours of the 17th thought out his plans
for the future. Ney had reported that the allied
force at Quatre Bras was not a detachment but an
army. Napoleon's cavalry, pushed forward in
pursuit of the Prussians, sent in accounts which indicated that they had retreated eastward, as, indeed, many stragglers and a few scattered units
had actually done. This was exactly in accord
with the Emperor's wishes. He decided to make
over thirty thousand men to Marshal Grouchy to
watch the Prussians and to lead the remainder of
his army against Wellington.

All through the night of the 16th the British and
allied troops kept streaming into Quatre Bras until the force there had risen to forty-five thousand
men. Wellington had received no news from
Gneisenau on the 16th, except a note to say that he
expected no great success from the fight at Ligny,
but hoped to hold his ground till nightfall. Early
on the morning of the 17th, therefore, the Duke
sent out a patrol in the direction of Ligny, which,
meeting the Prussian general in command of the

rearguard, brought intelligence of all that had happened. There was no sign of any movement on the enemy's part, so Wellington ordered the men to eat their breakfasts; and at nine o'clock there came a messenger from Blücher to announce that the Prussians would concentrate at Wavre, and to ask for Wellington's plans. The Duke answered that he should fall back to Mont St Jean, and, if supported by one Prussian corps, should there accept battle. He then gave the order for retreat; and the movement, screened with all the skill of which he was a master, began at ten o'clock. Hour after hour passed; the last of the infantry marched off, but still there was no sign of activity on Ney's side. As a matter of fact, Soult had left him all night long uninformed even of the result of the battle of Ligny. At last, at about one o'clock, parties of French horse struck against the British vedettes, and an hour later the French cavalry came forward in force. With the first cannon-shot fired by the British batteries there burst a terrific thunderstorm, with rain so heavy that all ground off the roads speedily became impassable. Through this deluge the British cavalry and horse-artillery retired with sundry little skirmishes and trifling loss to Mont St Jean. The French followed, their infantry not reaching their halting-places until dark, and in many cases until far into the night. The rain never ceased to pour down; the ground was covered for the most part with tall rye, wet as standing water; and, as usual, the French supply-service was defective. The men wandered about all night in search of food and shelter, plundering in all directions; and among the very worst offenders were the veterans of the Imperial Guard.

It was past one o'clock on the morning of the 18th before Wellington received Blücher's assurance that he would march to his assistance in the course of the day; but he did not then, nor even two hours later, count with certainty upon a decisive battle. Here at Waterloo he was in a position of his own selection, of which plans had been drawn up by his engineers months before; and he had so often defeated French frontal attacks in the Peninsula that he doubted if even Napoleon would care to repeat the experiment. The occupation of Brussels by the French might very well bring about the fall of the British Ministry, which was, perhaps, the prime object of the Emperor. He might, therefore, simply make a demonstration in front of Wellington, and move his main force round his right flank upon Brussels; and to foil such a manœuvre Wellington stationed from fifteen to eighteen thousand men at Hal, eleven miles to west of Waterloo, where they remained useless all day. As a matter of fact, both Soult and Reille counselled caution to Napoleon, and Reille recommended manœuvring in preference to a frontal attack; but the Emperor would not listen. By turning Wellington's position by the west, he would cut him off from his base on the sea; but, on the other hand, he would drive him straight into the arms of the Prussians, which was just what the Emperor wished to avoid. He could not, in fact, by one and the same manœuvre sever the British from their base and from Blücher.

On the Prussian side, Blücher was staunch in his purpose of leading his army to Wellington's support, but Gneisenau did his best, behind his back, to upset the agreement between them. He also selected the Prussian corps that lay remotest from Waterloo to proceed thither, and made such arrangements for their march as ensured delay for several hours, and this at a crisis when every moment was precious. It was not Gneisenau's fault that the battle of Waterloo was not lost.

On the French side, Napoleon was confident. He had about seventy thousand men, homogeneous and devoted to him, with two hundred and twenty-four guns. Wellington had about sixty-three thousand, composed of five different elements; and of these the Netherlanders, who numbered about seventeen thousand, were mostly of little value. His artillery counted one hundred and fifty-six pieces, and he had no guns of equal calibre and range to the best of the French. Napoleon designed to break through Wellington's centre, where stood the farmhouse of La Haye Sainte, and had disposed his best troops accordingly. Wellington was most fearful for his right, which rested on the much larger building of Hougoumont, and had placed the best of his troops there. As events turned out, the battle was fought more nearly according to Wellington's preconception than Napoleon's.

The Emperor had fixed the time for his great attack for one o'clock in the afternoon; the lateness of the hour being generally ascribed to his wish to give time for the sodden ground to dry. It is, however, more probable that he could not get his army together earlier, for discipline was hardly existent in it, and his Provost-Marshal had on the previous day actually resigned his position in despair. However, it was always his practice to make a bustle along the whole length of his enemy's line before delivering his real attack, and, accordingly, at eleven o'clock he made a demonstration against both of Wellington's flanks. His brother, Jerome, however, turned the assault upon Hougoumont into a serious affair, and, being repulsed in his first attempt, wasted thousands of men in further ineffectual efforts to storm this stronghold. Here was one blunder, the kind of blunder which occurs in every battle, that worked against Napoleon's plans.

At one o'clock came the first alarm of the approach of the Prussians, the heads of whose columns were visible five or six miles away. Napoleon detached eleven thousand men and thirty-two guns to deal with them, and then, under cover of a terrific cannonade from eighty massed pieces, he launched four divisions—some sixteen thousand men—in dense columns to the assault of Wellington's centre. These seemed to have carried the position, when two brigades of British cavalry, about two thousand strong, plunged into the middle of them, shattered them to fragments and hunted them back as a mere disorganized rabble. The cavalry, pursuing too far, were in their turn almost annihilated, but the moral effect of the charge was very great.

Napoleon now reinforced his artillery, and delivered another half-hearted attack on the centre, which was repulsed by the British infantry. Wellington, however, to protect his men from the rain of shot and shell, had drawn them back for a hundred yards, and Marshal Ney, mistaking this movement for the beginning of a retreat, turned a whole corps of cavalry upon them. The British infantry formed squares; the British gunners fired to the last moment, then took off the near wheel of each gun, and ran, bowling the wheels before them, into the nearest square. This attack was beaten off, and many more of the same nature, with heavy loss, the gunners trundling back the wheels and reopening fire as soon as they could safely do so.

Ney then mingled horse-artillery and infantry with his cavalry, which made the trial for the British squares far harder to bear; but still the squares stood firm. Then another assault was delivered on La Haye Sainte and repulsed. It was now six o'clock; the advance of the Prussians, though checked by the French, was beginning to make itself felt on the Emperor's right, and Napoleon, realising that matters were becoming serious, ordered a counter-attack on the Prussians and bade Ney take La Haye Sainte at all costs. This time at last Ney succeeded. A gap was opened and slowly widening in Wellington's centre; but it was closed by a brigade of British cavalry and by five raw Brunswick battalions, who ran away at first in a body, but under the magic of Wellington's personal leadership came forward again. And so a very dangerous crisis was successfully passed.

It was now seven o'clock, and Napoleon saw that it was time for a supreme effort. He launched five battalions of the Imperial Guard in dense columns to a final assault. They were shivered to pieces by the British infantry in line; and Wellington galloping from end to end of his array gave the order for a general counter-attack. He raised his hat as a signal, and the line, which had seemed so long rooted to the ground, broke into a majestic advance. The French gave way at every point. The Prussians took up the pursuit, and within twelve hours the French Army of Waterloo, had, as a military body, ceased to exist.

The victory was all Wellington's own. He showed extraordinary nerve in accepting battle at all with so infamous an army, and it was only the inspiration of his presence and personality which kept his troops to their work. At times even he failed. Whole battalions of Netherlanders van-

[241]

ished from the field; but the rest, Hanoverians, Brunswickers, British, stood firm. Wherever danger was greatest he was on the spot, serene and confident, on his thoroughbred chestnut horse. And, when there was a lull, he would send his staff to the reverse slope of the position, ride forward with a single aide-de-camp and stand in the full tempest of shot and shell with his telescope to his eye, watching and deciding. Possibly the consciousness that, in all good faith, he had given the German staff an inaccurate report of the position of his army, may have spurred him to unusual exertions; but certain it is that, but for him, the allied line would never have endured to the end. "It has been a damned nice thing," he said to Creevey next day, "the nearest-run thing that ever you saw in your life. By God, I don't think that it would have done if I had not been there." He said later that he personally had saved the battle four times, but in truth he saved it from the first shot to the last. The real miracle which he wrought was in making raw levies stand under the terrible fire of Napoleon's artillery. They would gladly have advanced; but he prevailed with them to emulate his own patience until the supreme moment should come.

He rode back to Brussels with what was left of his staff, silently, at a walk, one and all of the party wearing the aspect of a funeral train rather than of victory. As he dismounted he patted his thoroughbred chestnut, Copenhagen, approvingly on the quarter, and the horse, still fresh after fourteen or fifteen hours of hard work, lashed out with his near hind leg and narrowly missed making a casualty of the Commander-in-Chief. The list of his losses was brought to him, and before half of the names had been read to him, he broke down and cried. But there were a thousand matters to be looked to; and at one o'clock on the morning of the 19th a weary staff-officer rode out from Brussels with an order for the troops to march westward to Nivelles, the first stage on the road to Paris.

There was a trifling engagement on the 23rd, when Cambrai was carried by escalade; but most of the Duke's troubles arose from the infamous behaviour of the Netherlanders and the Prussians to the inhabitants when on the march. The Netherlanders were neither more nor less than a gang of robbers; and not only the men, but the officers of all nations except the British, entertained, as Wellington put it, the strongest objections to

anything like discipline and order. By the 6th of
July the Prussians were within Paris, while Wellington stayed outside. Blücher wished to levy a
huge contribution and to destroy the bridge of
Jena, but Wellington persuaded him to defer the
contribution until the allied sovereigns should arrive, and posted a British sentry on the bridge,
which, however, none the less owed its preservation
to the fact that the Prussian engineers lacked the
skill to blow it up. Everywhere Wellington's hand
was to be found working for mercy and moderation.
And then came the bitter battle between the diplomatists over the terms of peace; Prussia and the
German states clamouring for the dismemberment
of France and for a gigantic indemnity, while the
Tsar, Castlereagh, and Wellington earnestly with-
stood them and prevailed. Wellington had always
a warm corner for France in his heart, and no ani-
mosity even against Napoleon, whom he thought by
no means a bad governor of that country, if he
would leave other nations alone. But he was
wise enough to know that to humiliate and oppress
the French would be only to sow the seeds of future
wars, and he would be no party to such folly.

It was finally arranged that France should pay a
total indemnity of twenty-eight millions sterling,

and that for five years she should bear the expense of an army of occupation, made up of troops of nine different nations to the total of one hundred and fifty thousand men. To the supreme command of this army Wellington was appointed, a great position with great emoluments, which none the less he wrought steadily and strenuously to bring to an end as soon as possible. For the lighter side of his life, in his headquarters at Cambrai, it is enough to say that he kept a pack of hounds; as to the more serious side, it was his constant effort to make the burden of the army lie as lightly as might be upon the inhabitants; and he called upon the British Army to set the example of gentleness, courtesy, and general good behaviour. "We are Englishmen," he said, "and pride ourselves upon our deportment, and that pride shall not be injured in my keeping"; and woe to the officer or man who was guilty of harshness or oppression. So severe was he to all offences of this kind as to earn him not a little unpopularity, but he cared nothing for that. Meanwhile, his advice was sought by Ministers on every important question of foreign politics, and his correspondence was of astonishing variety and volume. In 1817 he was placed at the head of a commission which for two years had striven in vain to adjust the conflicting financial claims of the Allies upon France and the counter-claims of France upon the Allies; and after enormous labour he not only arrived at a satisfactory settlement, but negotiated for France a loan to enable her to meet her liabilities. Finally the army of occupation, not a little owing to his advice, was withdrawn from France after little more than three out of the appointed five years had expired; and in a farewell order he thanked the British troops for "the example which they had given to others by their own good conduct." During this time, 1815 to 1818, two attempts were made upon his life by Frenchmen; but, after the lapse of a century, French historians now confess that his dealings with their country were marked not only by wisdom and moderation but by generosity.

CHAPTER VIII

IN 1818, therefore, Wellington at last returned home to an England overclouded by stagnation in every trade, want of employment in every calling, and general distress. Naturally discontent was abroad, of which agitators took the usual advantage to make mischief; and the country was only deterred from a dangerous rising by stern repressive measures of the Government, which, happily, had the courage to enforce order and discipline. Immediately upon his arrival, Wellington was invited to join the Cabinet as Master-General of the Ordnance, which he consented to do with no great willingness. His time was taken up very much by thinking out plans for the defence of Canada and other colonies, but he also drew up a scheme for the distribution of the troops at home in case of an insurrection. His administration of the office itself was superlatively good. He reorganised it upon the lines laid down by James II and Marlborough, and by sheer thrift and good management gradually effected savings to the amount of two hundred thousand pounds a year. Thus he

[247]

was enabled to carry out two great and beneficial changes in the army. First, he made drivers of the artillery, which hitherto had been a distinct body, into an essential part of the regiment, laying down that all recruits of the artillery should henceforward be enlisted as both gunners and drivers. Secondly, he put an end to the odious system under which, even in hot climates, British soldiers had been huddled together by fours in wooden cribs, and gave each man an iron bedstead to himself. This was a homely matter, but the difference that it made to the soldiers' health, comfort, and self-respect was incalculable.

In 1826 the Duke of York, who had rendered inestimable service in restoring the discipline and organisation of the army, died after a long illness; and Wellington was appointed to succeed him as Commander-in-Chief, holding the office in conjunction with that of Master-General of the Ordnance, but drawing the salary of one only of the two posts. There was, as a matter of fact, little visible army to command, for the House of Commons had been steadily whittling it away ever since 1815, and there were not nearly men enough to do the work of the Empire. Of eighty-three infantry regiments of the Line in this year, fifty-one were on foreign service, five on passage home, twenty-three in Ireland, and only four in Great Britain. It was necessary at the close of 1826 to send five thousand troops to Portugal to support the reigning dynasty against a threatened military revolt, but even this small number could not be furnished without sending two battalions of Guards from England and withdrawing two battalions of the Line from Gibraltar. It is noteworthy that, before this expedition started, Wellington drew up for it a table of instructions as to transport and supply, just as he had done when he landed in the Mondego in 1808.

In 1827 the Prime Minister, Lord Liverpool, died, and was succeeded by Canning, under whom Wellington declined to serve; and the Duke therefore resigned his post. There is little profit in discussing the quarrel between the two men. There may or may not have been just ground for it, but they were in character absolutely antipathetic; Canning, brilliant, witty, egoistic, and not always quite straightforward, a typical politician; and Wellington, setting always duty before himself, full of plain common sense, and abhorring all intrigue. Canning died on the 8th of August, and was succeeded for a few months by Lord Goderich, under whom Wellington consented to resume the Commandership-in-Chief; but Goderich soon proved himself to be too small for the place; and in January 1828 Wellington himself consented to become Prime Minister and to form a new Government.

It is quite impossible to enter here into the details of foreign and domestic politics; and it must suffice to say that all over Europe there was distress owing to the exhaustion caused by the war, and therefore discontent, which, with the recent example of the French Revolution before the eyes of all, tended everywhere to vent itself in open or secret hostility to the established Government. Equally, all established governments, terrified by the fate of Louis XVI, were disposed to employ a high hand in dealing with this discontent. As a matter of fact, the trouble was one which time and patience only could remedy, and no government, whether popular or despotic or revolutionary, could even alleviate. But the general unrest was aggravated in some instances by certain of the settlements agreed upon in the final treaty of peace after Waterloo, which weighed heavily upon the parties concerned, and kept the foreign offices of Europe in constant anxiety. With all these difficulties Castlereagh had wrestled, not without success, until the strain wore him out, and he died by his own hand in 1822.

Wellington's knowledge of foreign politics, particularly in respect of France, Spain, and Portugal, was, through his past experience, peculiarly intimate, and on Castlereagh's death he had been appointed to represent England at the Congress of Verona for the settlement of divers outstanding matters in respect of Italy and Spain. Again, in 1827, he had been sent to Russia, nominally to congratulate the newly crowned Tsar, Nicholas, on his succession, but in reality to come to an understanding upon the question of Greek independence. In general, it was Wellington's principle to avoid all foreign entanglements, because he knew that England had no army with which to enforce her will, even if she wished to intervene. But in view of Russia's steady advance eastward he deprecated undue weakening of Turkey in the east, or of France in the west. For the rest, though by no means favourable to despotism as such, he was very shy of weakening established authority, and therefore of countenancing popular movements in other countries. He thought that foreign countries should settle for themselves the manner of their government, and had no taste for encouraging insurrections or lecturing to foreign potentates on the beauties of the English constitution. Being one who had travelled far, lived long in many foreign lands, and transacted business with many foreign officials, his outlook was infinitely broader and his sympathies infinitely wider than those of the most highly educated British politician. He knew his geography, also, which, not quite inexcusably owing to the want of good maps, was a rare accomplishment in those days.

For these very reasons he was out of his element with domestic politics, despite of his short career in the English House of Commons. He had learned, through bitter experience of the mischief that may be done by factious opposition, to hate and distrust political parties at large, which, though intelligible and even commendable, was not the best training for conducting government according to the party system. The prominent questions before the country, mostly arising out of the prevailing distress, were the condition of Ireland, with which was closely associated the removal of disabilities imposed upon Roman Catholics; amendment of the old commercial code of close trade within the Empire, with which was closely bound up the fate of British agriculture; and Parliamentary reform. On the Roman Catholic question Wellington had long been favourably inclined to emancipation, as it was called; as to the commercial code, he would have had food as cheap as might be consistently with British agricultural prosperity; as to Parliamentary reform, he considered that the existing system, with its curious mixture of venal and proprietary boroughs on one hand, and boroughs with manhood suffrage on the other, could not be improved upon. Concerning the first, he himself carried Catholic Emancipation, thereby alienating and breaking up his party, and destroying his own political reputation. Also twenty years later the old commercial code, which he had upheld, was utterly abolished. Free Trade, as it is called, was substituted for Protection, with the result that British agriculture was ruined, and the country brought into the greatest danger during the German War. In Parliamentary reform, which was trumpeted forth by the Whigs as the nostrum that should put an end to all distress, Wellington reposed no faith, and was not afraid to say so.

In truth, it was in the working of the Parliamentary machine that he showed himself principally defective. He expected his party to be a body of disciplined men, and his Cabinet to be a group of obedient subordinates, like his divisional generals, all obeying his orders as Commander-in-Chief without delay and without question. His gift of clear insight and his training in swift decision were out of place in a Cabinet, which, like any other large committee, usually contains its proportion of timid and irresolute men, some of them able, some of them stupid, but all alike averse from being hurried and committed against their will.

Nevertheless the Duke's short administration produced one measure of supreme importance, namely, the Act for the establishment of the Metropolitan Police, which was the parent of the entire constabulary of Great Britain. This was, in truth, a military measure, and the most important military measure, perhaps, that ever was passed in these islands, for it set up a standing army for the enforcement of the law, and, by relieving the regular forces of the very invidious duty of preserving order at home, set them free to act as the police of the Empire. Little though many of us may realise the fact, we owe it to Wellington that we can go about our daily avocations unarmed; and this is a far more important privilege than that of casting a vote for a representative in Parliament or in local governing bodies. The Metropolitan Police Force thus made in 1829 was composed to a great extent of disbanded soldiers; and there never were constables more trustworthy nor non-commissioned officers so steady. In 1830 this good work was supplemented by the foundation of the Irish Constabulary, which, so long as it received loyal support from its masters, had not a peer in Europe, with the possible exception of the Carabinieri of Spain.

By the end of 1830 the Duke had been driven from office, and then followed the long and weary battle over Reform, which to us in these days makes such strange reading. The misery in the country had never been more acute, and there was consequently dangerous discontent, agitation, and violence. Cholera also made its appearance in London in 1832; and altogether there was enough trouble to try the patience of the most orderly nation. But how the ailment was to be remedied by placing political power in the hands of petty shopkeepers, it is difficult to see. However, a great majority were satisfied that the millennium would follow upon the passing of such a measure, and Wellington, who uncompromisingly opposed

it, felt the wrath of the mob. The windows of
Apsley House were broken, and in the autumn of
1831 the house was constantly surrounded by a
yelling rabble which followed him wherever he
went. On the anniversary of Waterloo he was
attacked in the streets of London, and but for the
presence of two old soldiers, who joined him and
marched by his stirrups to prevent him from being
tilted out of his saddle, he would probably have
been murdered. Such demonstrations he treated
with absolute indifference, though he placed Apsley
House in a state of defence, and when travelling carried with him loaded pistols. The popu-
lace is seldom formidable unless it is unopposed.

Not through intimidation, but through convic-
tion that the Reform Bill must be passed lest a
worse thing should befall, was the Duke at length
constrained to give way, with such awkward grace
as is possible to one who had repeatedly declared
that the measure would mean the ruin to the
country. Yet, though his prophecy was falsified,
he saw more deeply into the heart of the matter
than the reformers. The country was not ruined;
but there was no return of prosperity nor abate-
ment of the revolutionary spirit until 1849, and
then the change was due not to any legislative

enactment but to a mere accident—the discovery of great quantities of gold in California and Australia. The promoters of the Reform Bill declared that it would be final. Wellington was under no such illusion. All reform, he said, would end in being radical; and since 1832 the franchise has been repeatedly lowered until it has become the right, practically, of every grown man and woman. Yet democracy, as it is called, has not killed the revolutionary spirit. We, in this year 1925, are passing through a long period of depression analogous to that which overclouded England for a full generation after Waterloo; and, as usual, the remedy is sought in violent constitutional or unconstitutional changes. But whether any of them can prove to be an effective cure is quite another matter.

The Ministry of Lord Grey, which had come in after the passing of the Reform Bill, soon fell from power, and in November Wellington was summoned by the King to form a new administration. He put forward for Prime Minister the name of Sir Robert Peel, who was abroad, and until his return actually did for four weeks the work of all the Secretaries of State, finally taking over the Foreign Office for the two months during which the new administration lasted. Not until 1841 was he again in office, and then once more under the leadership of Sir Robert Peel, but without a portfolio. He was by that time much aged. Since 1826 he had suffered from deafness, having wholly lost the use of one ear through mistreatment by a surgeon; and in November 1839 he had an alarming seizure which left him weakened and bent, though with intellect unimpaired. His principal political work lay in the House of Lords, where he sat patiently day after day from beginning to end of the sitting, listening, or endeavouring to listen, to every word—a pathetic instance of his devotion to duty. Once again he was fated to sacrifice the convictions of a lifetime upon public grounds, and to support Sir Robert Peel in repealing the Corn Laws and introducing complete free trade in corn. "A good Government for this country is more important than Corn Laws or any other consideration," he wrote. He conceived Peel's to be such a Government, and, acting upon that opinion, carried the measure through the Lords. Almost immediately afterwards Peel was defeated by a combination of his former supporters and his constant opponents; and the good Government came to an abrupt end.

WELLINGTON

At the request of the Queen, Wellington retained the post of Commander-in-Chief, which had been given to him by patent in 1842, but he was now failing rapidly. His subordinates loyally kept the secrets of the Horse Guards to themselves, but it was whispered that the Duke, as is the way with old men, was constantly dropping off to sleep in the midst of business, and that in the general conduct of affairs he was difficult and intractable. Anonymous publications of officers, who, with or without reason, felt themselves aggrieved, betrayed something of the truth; but all the old reverence for "the Duke" had returned, and none would venture to speak openly. His military secretary, Lord Fitzroy Somerset, who had served with him in the Peninsula and at Waterloo, was the most skilful of his staff in managing him, and stood with loyal devotion between him and all difficulties and dislikes; for Lord Fitzroy happily possessed a sweetness of temper and a gentle courtesy which endeared him equally to the oldest veteran and the newly commissioned ensign. At times the Duke was his old self; and, when a Government of his political opponents sought his advice for the protection of London against the threatened Chartist insurrection in 1848, the old man's eyes sparkled with joy at a return to his old work, and he made masterly dispositions for safeguarding every important point without showing a single red-coat either to frighten the friendly or to provoke the hostile. His bearing gave confidence to a nervous Cabinet, and his precautions brought the dreaded insurrection to naught.

In 1850 he urged that the Prince Consort should take over the Commandership-in-Chief of the army, advice which the Prince wisely rejected; and the Duke retained the office to the end. Physically he was still equal to exertions which were extraordinary for one of his advanced age, and mentally he was still full of his old common sense. On his eighty-third birthday, the 1st of May 1852, he was a guest at the annual dinner of the Royal Academy. "We drank his health with immense shouting and table-banging," wrote Macaulay in his journal. "He returned thanks and spoke of the loss of the *Birkenhead*. I remarked (and Lawrence, the American Minister, said that he had remarked the same thing) that in his eulogy of the poor fellows who were lost, the Duke never spoke of their courage, but of their subordination and discipline. He said this several times." Well might he say it a dozen times; for the example of the men in the *Birkenhead* has nerved not troops only, but British men and women from the highest to the lowest, to face disaster at sea without panic; and the discipline which ensured it was principally of the Duke's own making.

In the early autumn of the same year he made his last speech in the House of Lords, fortunately upon a military topic—the reconstitution of the militia,—a speech full of good sense, in which he paid a generous and graceful tribute to the Hanoverian militia who fought at Waterloo. Actually the last words that he spoke in the House were to move for a return of the troops in the *Birkenhead*. He went to Walmer Castle, as usual, at the end of the Session. On the 13th of September he was in excellent health and spirits, and made appointments for the morrow. On the morning of the 14th his servant called him soon after six o'clock, but the Duke did not rise. The servant returned an hour later, and the Duke complained of feeling very ill, beckoned that he should be moved into his armchair, and then fell asleep and woke no more.

The only precedent for the burial of so great a man was that of the Duke of Marlborough, and accordingly a huge, ponderous, florid car was constructed to carry one who would much have preferred a simple gun-carriage, to his grave. Representatives of every regiment in the army followed him in long procession from Chelsea Hospital; and in St. Paul's Cathedral, by the side of Nelson, the great Duke was laid to his rest.

CHAPTER IX

THERE now remains the difficult task of summarising the work of this long and eventful life, and of deducing from it the salient features of Wellington's character and personality. And first we must note that nature had withheld from him a gift with which she had endowed the two men with whom he is most frequently compared, Marlborough and Napoleon—the gift of personal charm, enhanced by personal beauty. Napoleon's face is too well known to need description. Marlborough's noble features are disguised in most portraits by the hideous wig which was the fashion of his time, and can only be justly studied through the bust which shows him with his own short hair. But his godlike serenity and his irresistible charm are proverbial; and Napoleon, though he frequently lapsed into vulgar outbursts of temper, could, when he chose, be equally fascinating.[1] Both could attract and win over even the most hostile by sheer delightfulness; and both were worshipped

[1] The author's grandfather twice had long conversations with Napoleon at Elba, and left behind him an oral tradition of the Emperor's personal charm.

by the humblest men who served under them. A
smile from either of them sufficed to lift into the
seventh heaven, and a word of praise could banish
the grievances of a lifetime. Charm backed by
genius is the most powerful combination to be
found among mortal men.

Wellington was not as they were. In person he
was not uncomely; but his features, with the wavy
black hair, fine blue eyes rather deeply sunk,
aquiline nose, immensely strong jaw and pointed
chin, indicated above all things, character. The
mouth was rather disproportionately small; and it
should seem that up to the age of forty-two or three
the lips, owing to prominent upper teeth, did not
close firmly,[1] but that later the upper lip, which
was very thin, ran down in a point to join the
lower. But it was not a kind or sympathetic
mouth. His voice has been handed down by tradition as deep, gruff, and rather thick, but the
last-named quality may have come late and been

---

[1] This peculiarity does not appear in Hoppner's portrait, painted
while he was Sir Arthur Wellesley, but it is plainly to be seen
in Goya's portrait, painted in Spain, and this is confirmed by
a water-colour drawing, dated 1809, by Denis Dighton, which shows
him with what is called a rabbit-mouth, the two central incisor
teeth of the upper jaw being very prominent. These teeth seem
to have receded or, possibly, to have been lost before Wellington's
return to England.

due to deafness.[1] He was five feet nine inches in height, spare, muscular, very well made, with a step of remarkable firmness and elasticity—in fact, a man who moved well, quickly, and resolutely. His feet were small; and his hands, with slender taper fingers, the hands of an artist. In old age he became bowed, and very thin, but never wholly lost his white hair. He was scrupulously neat and smart in his dress, for, having a good figure, he was not above making the best of it, and one of his nicknames was the *Beau*. In common with most men of his age he necessarily spent many hours of the day, whether in peace or war, on horseback. He had a bad and ugly seat in the saddle, sitting very far back, with the space from hip-joint to knee almost parallel to the ground; and thus when hunting he had frequent falls. If we are to believe the caricaturists, he was once ignobly thrown when reviewing the Grenadier Guards, of which he was latterly colonel. It is curious that a well-built man, who must have ridden tens of thousands of miles, should never have improved this defect.

Shyness and self-repression were, as has already

[1] I have heard more than one man reproduce his voice, but none of them of course knew him except in old age.

been told, the keys of his character in youth; and he seems never to have impressed strangers greatly at first sight. Nelson, whom he met once in a Minister's ante-room, talked inflated nonsense to him until he found out that he was the successful general, Sir Arthur Wellesley, when he changed his tone abruptly; and a foreigner, Count Molé, who knew him first after Waterloo, passed the following remarkable judgment. "Wellington's intelligence is, if anything, below the average, and his education even inferior to his intelligence. He can neither talk nor write. Add to this a taste for women . . . and a thirst for the pettiest amusements; this at the first glance was my impression of the Duke of Wellington. But one must get beneath the surface to the character and will of the man to find the secret of his glory and his life. He possesses that imperturbable will, which, calm and constant, wears down all resistance. No obstacle surprises him; no difficulty deters him. . . . His good sense is almost infallible. Seeking after truth, loving justice, he repels the evil and the false even as instruments of success. He sees things, so to speak, face to face, less by superiority of intelligence than by clear-sightedness. He does not dominate them; he sees them as they are. Men

would have less scorn for uprightness and good
sense, if they knew how they make for success.
How many times have I seen the Duke of Wellington evade a trap set for him, outwit the most cunning, deceive the cleverest."

In brief, Wellington's real gift was transcendent
common sense, the rare power (shared also by
Marlborough) of seeing things as they are, which,
whether it be granted to soldier, statesman, or
artist, signifies genius. Those who possess this
insight see clearly at a glance many things that
puzzle other men. Seeing clearly they can decide
promptly, and deciding promptly they can act immediately. Add to this endowment inexhaustible
patience, unwearied industry, and absolute straight-
forwardness and integrity; and there is a combination of human forces which must carry a man very
far. Such a combination was found in Wellington.

He was fortunate in going to India when he did,
where there was abundance of work to his hand,
and where, when he was not practically an independent sovereign, he could work his will in many
matters through his brother, the Governor-
General. The climate suited him; his physical
health improved; and his energy found scope
in every detail of administration, which widened

his experience and ripened his powers. Even
Oriental guile became transparent to the piercing eye which saw things as they were; and old
officials, who had lived in India for years, found
that the newcomer, Arthur Wellesley, could match
himself successfully, as they could never hope to
do, against the subtlest intrigues of the Mahratta.
He could teach them much also in the handling of
the native inhabitants of India.   It does not appear
that he was in the slightest degree attracted by the
character of the said natives, by the romance of
their past history, or by anything that concerned
them.   I cannot recall that he ever mentioned, in
later life, his Indian servants, who were probably
faithful enough and devoted to the "Bara Sahib."
But he found himself charged with the duty of
ending anarchy, putting down disorder, and root-
ing out injustice and oppression, which were the
four things that he hated most in the world, and
he did his work with unswerving honesty and
uprightness.   Those strenuous years in India were,
I suspect, the happiest of his life.   Probably he
varied his task with sport from time to time, for he
was a good shot with a fowling-piece; but we hear
nothing of a day with snipe or duck, of spearing
hogs or shooting tigers.   Nevertheless I think that

I find in his letters from India a geniality, possibly due to comparative youth, which disappears from those of later times. White men were so few that, even though most of them were (as he says) ill-tempered, they were less unacceptable than they would have been at home; and there were some whom he evidently both liked and respected. Of few men in the whole course of his life does he speak with warmer admiration than of Colonel Barry Close; and it is possible that he did not meet with many who were really abler. Even Talley-rand he compared with a wily old Mahratta, by no means to the disadvantage of the Mahratta.

From the highest and most responsible positions, both civil and military, in India, he returned to take up quite subordinate posts in Europe, ful-filling them always with the same quiet sense of duty until the time came for him to take command in Portugal. In his whole career he gave no more signal example of his power to see things as they are than during this last period. It is true that he needed the experience of that campaign of 1809 to teach him the ways of the Spaniards; but, hav-ing once learned them, he turned both the virtues and defects of that wonderful people to the best account. No ordinary man would have seen al-

[269]

most at a glance that, so long as he could hold
Lisbon and put forty thousand men into the field
with an efficient service of transport and supply, he
could relax, and eventually shake off, the hold of
three hundred thousand French upon the Peninsula.
A war of attrition is necessarily a long war; but
in Spain, at any rate, the method was sure. It
was afterwards reckoned that the losses of the
French in the Peninsula averaged one hundred
dead a day, not necessarily killed in action, but
dead through starvation, fatigue, exposure, sickness, and assassination. In five years the number
would amount to over one hundred and seventy
thousand, not mere casualties but corpses.

But to maintain this war of attrition it was
necessary to keep the army in a high state of
efficiency; and a great part of that army, it must
be remembered, was Portuguese. This involved
a very large share in the administration of Portugal itself, in the face of much jealousy and obstruction; but with the help, happily, of Mr. Villiers
Stuart, the very able British Minister at Lisbon,
and one Portuguese statesman, who was both loyal
and capable, Forjaz, he was successful. The
difficulties of the situation were augmented, first,
by lack of money and the cost of exchange, which,

it may be repeated, was twenty-five per cent. against in England, and secondly, by the insecurity of the Government in Downing Street. It was almost imperative to give Ministers a victory in the *Gazette* from time to time in order to justify their courage and resolution in pursuing their policy of fighting in the Peninsula. Thus there lay upon Wellington always a triple load of anxiety, to demand sacrifices of the Portuguese; to ensure, so far as in him lay, that the Ministry in London should not fall lest a new Ministry should turn those sacrifices to naught; and, as a means to those ends, to keep his army efficient and well equipped without money.

In the matter of the army, he was grievously handicapped by three special disadvantages. First and foremost there was the difficulty of enforcing discipline, only overcome at last by the importation of a lawyer. And here it must be noted that Wellington instituted for the first time in the history of the army a military police corps. We owe, as a matter of fate, both our civil and our military police to him, and such a service would of itself be sufficient to make fame for any other man.

Next, there was the problem of transport and supply, rendered the harder of solution by many contributory causes, of which the principal were the inexperience of the Commissaries and the miserable nature of the Portuguese roads. By sheer hard work, however, he organised a transport system of pack-mules; he found an admirable Chief Commissary in Sir Robert Kennedy; and the earliest work, so far as I know—certainly the earliest useful work,—upon the duties of what is now called the Army Service Corps, came from the pen of one of the subordinate Commissaries, Mr. Bisset. One difficulty in the conduct of this pack-mule transport was sufficiently curious. The muleteers were all of them hired Spaniards who worked willingly enough, on credit, for the British, but declined to do anything for the Portuguese, whom they held in supreme contempt. This is the kind of complication, so common in war, that upsets all reckonings and is absolutely unintelligible to a War Office though embarrassing enough to a Commander-in-Chief. Let it meanwhile be noted that when Wellington's transport and supply system failed on the retreat from Burgos, the Chief Commissary, Kennedy, was absent, and his place had been taken by one of imperfect knowledge and skill. But for this accident there would have been no failure.

Lastly, there were the defects of the medical service. One of Wellington's worst troubles was with convalescent men from the central hospital at Belem, near Lisbon, who were necessarily sent up to rejoin their regiments in small parties, and made their way, not necessarily to the front, plundering and robbing all over the country. This was ended by Dr. Mcgrigor, who was as good a man in his own line as Kennedy, and who, with Wellington's full sanction and encouragement, altered the whole system of hospitals, with vast improvements both to the health and discipline of the men. This Mcgrigor, afterwards Sir James, was the father of British military hygiene, which also sprang into life in Wellington's army. Of course the surgery of the time was still crude, according to modern notions, and the sufferings of the wounded were very great; but the only spring-waggons of the army—those of the Royal Waggon Train,—though intended for general transport work, were used exclusively for sick and wounded men, and so were the germ of the modern ambulance.

A word must be added as to the spiritual needs of the army. Chaplains had originally been, like the regimental surgeons, practically the servants of the colonels, but it had become the practice of the colonels to dispense with a chaplain, and to pay his salary to any friend in holy orders who might welcome a little addition to his income. Many fairly large expeditions went abroad without any chaplain at all, and Wellington in 1811 found himself with only one—an excellent man—in his whole army. The result was the rise of Methodist preachers both among officers and men; and Wellington, though by no means disapproving of this in the abstract, thought it bad for discipline that private soldiers should preach sermons against the failings of their officers. He therefore begged for more chaplains, and more chaplains came. They were not, as a body, a great success; but there was at least one who insisted upon accompanying the troops into the firing-line, and his example has since found many followers.

I pass now to more general military considerations, and first to the executive officers of the army. At the outset Wellington had much trouble not only with his generals but with all ranks of the regimental officer. We have seen how he complained of having to do the work of every divisional general; and, even when he had gradually purged out the incompetent—and they were many,—he still could not be sure that those that remained would obey orders. There was the flagrant case, during the retreat from Burgos, of three generals taking a route of their own instead of following that prescribed to them, which nearly led to disaster. On the other hand, these same generals always betrayed nervousness and helplessness when required to show any initiative, even as late as in the Pyrenees in 1813. None the less, such was the universal lack of discipline among all grades of officer, that Wellington always upheld the authority of these bad generals, spoke well of them in his despatches, and was chary of sending them home except on some specious pretext which could not be interpreted as disgrace. The most remarkable instance of this kind is that of Colonel Willoughby Gordon, who was sent out to Wellington in 1812 to take the place of his former Quartermaster-General, George Murray. Gordon was a very arrogant and self-sufficient man, and Wellington had been warned, further, that he was not to be trusted; but, not seeing how he could show lack of confidence in his chief staff-officer, Wellington kept no secrets from him. The result was that information, which could have been gleaned only from Wellington's most confidential despatches, appeared in the English newspapers; and the leak-

age could be traced to no one but Gordon. As
this officer further showed himself most incompetent
in the field, Wellington naturally longed to be rid
of him as soon as possible, but he could suggest
no means of doing so except by the offer to him
of a berth at the Horse Guards. The Duke of
York, when this was suggested to him, very
properly answered that he had no intention of providing high offices for men of proved inefficiency.
The matter led to a long correspondence between
Wellington and Sir Henry Torrens, the Duke of
York's right-hand man, who exerted much ingenuity to contrive that Gordon's removal should not
seem to be a deliberate recall. Fortune favoured
him by placing Gordon for a time on the sick-list.
Gordon went home as an invalid, and Torrens,
after an interview with him, left him mourning
over the disappointment which Wellington would
feel over the impossibility of his return. "He will
not go out again," wrote Torrens privately to
Wellington; and Gordon did not go out again.

This example shows how far Wellington was
prepared to go in shielding a senior officer from
public disgrace. But the principle which guided
him is plain. There was far too much open
criticism of superiors by inferiors to please him, and

more than once he visited the sins of careless generals upon good regimental officers. This was hard, sometimes cruelly hard; and the harder because when once he had pronounced judgment upon an individual, or even upon a regiment, he would never revoke it, no matter what facts might subsequently be brought to light. He would admit that, if he had known earlier of all the circumstances, he would have softened his censure, perhaps have spared it altogether; but, once declared, he would never recall it. And his condemnation would sometimes be sweeping, confounding the innocent with the guilty, as in the case of the entire army after the campaign of 1812, and of the artillery at Waterloo. Protests were useless. With him it was, "What I have written, I have written"; and there was no more to be said. He was not merely the commander, but the maker of an army; and he upheld the principle that a general officer could do no wrong in the eyes of his subordinates, and the commander-in-chief no wrong except in his own eyes. It is difficult to pass right judgment upon him without the knowledge which he possessed, and which in these days it is impossible for even the most learned to imagine, of the general spirit and tone of the army as it then was.

[277]

However, as the discipline of both men and officers improved, Wellington softened somewhat towards them. He seems never to have been very familiar with any of his generals, but held one and all aloof with Olympian majesty, partly from his natural shyness, partly from intellectual contempt. In his wrath he was terrible, particularly if anything underhand were in question. He reduced his adjutant-general, who was always intriguing and making mischief, to tears by a short lecture, and sent an unfortunate Spaniard almost fainting from his presence after an interview of a very few minutes. But it was not often that he stormed against offenders, preferring to use the biting sarcasm of which he was a master. Few of his generals tried him more constantly than Robert Craufurd, who though both cantankerous and disloyal, was none the less an admirable disciplinarian, and the greatest master of outpost-duty in the army; and Wellington, knowing his value, in spite of much provocation dealt leniently with him. "I am glad to see you safe, Craufurd," he said on one occasion, with meaning, after the Light Division had been with some difficulty extricated from serious peril, incurred through Craufurd's rashness. "Oh, I have been in no danger, I assure you," rejoined Craufurd hotly. "But I have," answered Wellington, a crushing retort which silenced even Craufurd. So, too, when the three generals disobeyed orders, as already mentioned, on the retreat from Burgos, Wellington gave them no more rebuke than a single withering sentence. When questioned afterwards as to the incident, his reply was, "Oh! by God, it was too serious to say anything."

Still, with all this power of sarcastic bitterness he was not ungenial nor unsympathetic. He would wave his staff-officers away on hunting mornings in Portugal, and ride among the foremost of the followers of the very primitive pack of the Peninsular Army. "Comfortable dogs! Let 'em alone," he said on another occasion when, in the course of the fighting in the Pyrenees, he came upon a battalion which had found plenty of food and drink and was settling down to a night of enjoyment. Moreover, if Harry Smith is to be trusted, Wellington seems to have unbent more to the promising young officers, who were to be generals of the future, than to the older men who were already of high rank—such young men as John Colborne, the future Lord Seaton, and Harry Smith himself. In fact he appears to have felt real sympathy with youth and its manifold frivolities, when they did not interfere with military duty, which explains Count Molé's reference to his "thirst for the pettiest amusements." He could and did soften when he felt safe to do so. My own impression is that he had actually an emotional nature, which he kept, owing to early training, under so stern control as to forbid it any vent except upon very rare occasions.

His personal staff have left no reminiscences of their relations with him. At the outset he was undoubtedly his own chief of staff, and worked out every detail himself. But George Murray, his Quartermaster-General, did more and more work after 1810, and his absence was sadly felt during the retreat from Burgos in 1812. Actually during the campaign of the Pyrenees, Murray took upon himself to issue orders—and very good orders— upon his own authority, without the slightest disapproval from his chief. In general, a subordinate who took upon himself to trench in the slightest degree upon the Commander-in-Chief's functions, did so at his peril. Even Mcgrigor got into trouble once in this way, though, by taking his own line, he spared much suffering and saved many lives to wounded men. But it would be a mistake to suppose that Wellington was fit to manage only what is called in modern slang a "one man show." He could work indefatigably at detail, but he was by no means its slave. He would take, on occasion, personal command of a division, a brigade, or even a battalion, but from the moment when he entered France with a really large force under his command, his mind and powers expanded and he confined his personal control to broad principles and great movements, leaving details to his subordinates.

It is the habit of foreign critics, few of whom have ever studied the Peninsular War, to belittle Wellington as a soldier, while conceding to him some praise as an organiser and an administrator. French writers, in particular, were in the habit of pointing out that the French generals only retreated before him because they lacked victuals; but they omit to emphasise the fact that Wellington was able to follow them up because he, through his own foresight, possessed what they lacked. To manœuvre in order to starve your enemy is one of the oldest operations of war; but there are more ways of doing this than by driving him into a desert or blockading him in a fortress, namely, by organising perfectly the service of transport and supply, and by paying for food requisitioned from the inhabitants, and by sternly repressing the extortion of provisions by force. These methods may not all of them have a military sound, but they accomplished military objects, which is the real point.

Any question as to Wellington's strategical ability, in the more commonly accepted sense, is decided by his great advance from Portugal and the turning of the line of the Ebro in 1814. He possessed one gift or remarkable value to a strategist, that of retaining the geography of a country clearly and accurately in his memory. Thus he could and did produce a sound and valuable memorandum upon the military position in India thirty years after he had left it, without a map before him. His tactical eye for ground was not less remarkable, and was aided by wonderful natural eyesight. It is perhaps as a tactician that he outdid the whole of his contemporaries. He was the only one who met column with line, and, when occupying a position on rising ground, invariably hid away his troops on the reverse slope. Herein he was helped by the character and the steadiness of the British soldier who prefers instinctively support on right and left to a following in rear, and who was proof against the greatest trial of the day, ricochet round-shot. His trick of concealing his troops made the French generals latterly very cautious; and it may well be that Ney at Quatre Bras was chary of putting forth his full strength at once, from recollection of Wellington's tactics in the Peninsula.

In the handling of cavalry Wellington was not so happy as with infantry. Indeed, he always complained that the British horse, except in small bodies, was unmanageable owing to its tendency to excessive speed. None the less it is certain that few more successful attacks of cavalry upon infantry are to be found in military history than those at Salamanca and Waterloo. With his artillery Wellington was never on the best of terms, and his handling of his guns has been much criticised, perhaps the more so because his great rival, Napoleon, was such a master in the wielding of that arm. Sufficient allowance, however, has never been made for the fact that he had, on the one hand, no heavier guns than nine-pounders, whereas the French had twelve-pounders; while, on the other, he possessed the new missile—shrapnel shell —which, as already explained, was equivalent to "long-range grape." These points are highly technical, and it were to be wished that some artillery officer would finally elucidate them and decide the question once for all. Meanwhile, it must be remembered that the gunners, being subject to the Master-General of the Ordnance and not to the Commander-in-Chief like the rest of the army, were a peculiar people, umbrageous, and not too easy to handle. With all Wellington's defects, however, it may be doubted whether Napoleon himself were his superior on the battlefield. He seemed to divine instinctively the moral strength and the limit of endurance, not only of his own troops, but of his enemy's, husbanding his reserves jealously and always throwing them in at the right moment. There is, perhaps no more striking example of this gauging of moral strength than the occasion of Colborne's counter-attack on the Imperial Guard at Waterloo. Colborne was an admirable and daring officer, but, after opening his counter-attack with signal success, he was about to halt, apprehending a possible onslaught of French cavalry. "Go on, Colborne, go on!" shouted Wellington. "Go on; they won't stand." He knew by instinct that the French had shot their last bolt.

On his return home after the withdrawal of the army of occupation, he is supposed to have kept his old comrades at a distance and neglected the army.

But it was no new thing for him to hold aloof from his generals, who, as a matter of fact, were not men of great intellect or very interesting character. On the other hand, he paid generous tribute in the House of Lords to the commanders in all the many campaigns which were fought between Waterloo and his death—to Archibald Campbell (an old officer of the Portuguese Army) in Burma, to John Colborne in Canada, to Hugh Gough in China, to Charles Napier in Scinde, and to Harry Smith in the Punjab. Once only did he pass withering criticism, namely, on the disastrous expedition to Afghanistan (1839–1842), which was so insanely misconducted by the Indian "politicals." In dealing with the later phrases of this war he abstained from mentioning names, substituting characteristically the phrase, "the gentleman who commanded the army," for that of the misguided and unfortunate political agent, Sir William Macnaghten. His real pupils were Charles Napier, John Colborne, and Harry Smith, and it is probable that he reckoned the first of these to be the best. It was to Charles Napier that he spoke the famous words, after the desperate battles in the Punjab, "If you don't go (to India), I must"; and though later, in the dispute between Charles

Napier, the Commander-in-Chief, and Dalhousie, the Governor-General, he decided on grounds of discipline against Napier, he received him on his arrival in England, in official disgrace, with unusual demonstrations of kindness and cordiality. "I thought he would have embraced me," wrote Napier to his brother William. So, too, when Colborne returned with honour from Canada, and Harry Smith was recalled from the Cape, Wellington himself proposed the health of each of them at the Waterloo banquet. To these three men, at any rate, the praise or censure of other men was as naught in comparison with the approval of the Duke; and it is doubtful whether England has produced, since the Duke, three greater soldiers.

As to neglect of the army, Wellington's work at the Ordnance Office, already mentioned, furnishes at least some answer; but it is constantly reproached against the Duke that he did not use, as he might have used, his great and irresistible influence to soften the hard lot of the British soldier after Waterloo. Now it must be confessed that the soldier was never worse treated than between 1815 and 1840. He was abominably housed, ridiculously fed, absurdly and unhealthily clothed, and, to an extent that is now hardly realised, sentenced to perpetual exile in unhealthy climates. But these were not matters within the cognizance of the Commander-in-Chief. Any reforms in these provinces signified the expenditure of money, and were the business of the Secretary at War and of Parliament; and there never was a time when the House of Commons showed more furious jealousy of military expenditure. During the short intervals when his party was in power the Duke secured real benefits for the British soldier. Thus, in 1831, through his Secretary at War, Sir Henry Hardinge, he improved very greatly the prospects of the private on his discharge, giving him not only a better pension, but direct encouragement to good behaviour with the colours. And Hardinge very ingeniously contrived to combine this reform with a saving of fifty thousand pounds on soldiers' pensions, not only without hardship, but with actual gain to all well-conducted men. But what was the result? A few years later the Whig Government disgracefully upset the whole arrangement in order to save a few pounds, drove a new and hard bargain with ignorant old soldiers, and ended by plunging themselves into a sea of dirty and costly troubles. When politicians, for the sake of flaunting a small economy on the estimates, would thus break faith with the soldier, it was hopeless for the most highly distinguished officers to strive to benefit him.

Moreover, it is a fallacy to suppose that the Whigs would have gladly accepted advice from Wellington. They hated him because his victories had kept the Tories so long in power. They were unwearied in attacking him in Parliament throughout almost the whole of the Peninsular War. His disloyal Quartermaster-General, Willoughby Gordon, was known to have promised to write from headquarters to Lord Grey; and I find it hard to forgive Lord Grey for thus abetting treachery in a staff-officer against his chief. Even after Waterloo they steadily belittled him, insinuating that he owed his success to others; and they betrayed childish vexation when Wellington's despatches were published, proving conclusively that all of his work was done by himself. So far were they from seeking his advice that they would not invite it, even upon the issue of a new drill-book which in itself was almost an insult. How could a proud and self-respecting man seek to influence a set of men whom in his heart he must have viewed, and viewed rightly, with unspeakable contempt? That Wellington approved

of the overcrowding and insanitary horrors of
the barracks and of the wretched monotonous
diet is not to be supposed for a moment, if only
because of the mortality thus caused in the army.
But even as Commander-in-Chief he was powerless
in such matters. So thorough was the subordination of the military to the civil element that, as he
himself put it, he could not move a corporal's
guard from London to Hounslow without a route,
or, in other words, without permission from the
Secretary at War. It was not for Wellington to
put himself in the position of receiving a snub from
some obscure politician whose loins were thinner
than his little finger. As to stirring up an agitation about military matters, such an idea would not
only have been instantly misconstrued by Parliament and the country, but would not have been
entertained for one second by Wellington himself.
He had far too strong a sense of discipline and of
his duty to uphold constitutional authority to
dream of such a thing; and anyone who ventured
to suggest it would have drawn upon himself a
tempest of wrathful indignation.

As a matter of fact, every measure taken to improve the lot of the private soldier has originated
in the first instance with regimental officers, and

[289]

only after long delay has been adopted by the War Office. Wellington in his time had been a keen regimental officer, very zealous, as his letters show, for the welfare, comfort, and health of his men, and thoroughly in sympathy with the regimental spirit, which was, and until very recently remained, the real life and breath of the army. Towards the end of his time in the Peninsula he was made Colonel of the Blues, and he at once put on the uniform and inspected the regiment, knowing the value and importance of such things. He laboured unceasingly and with ultimate success in the Peninsula to make the regimental officers look after their men; and to his inspiration in no small measure must be attributed the many methods of improving the soldier's lot which were thought out by regimental officers all over the world after Waterloo. It must be remembered, further, that it was Wellington who persuaded the War Office to establish a higher grade of non-commissioned officer than the sergeant, with increased pay, and that he was, in fact, the creator of the colour-sergeant and the troop-sergeant-major.

It is sometimes urged as a reproach against him that he opposed the abolition of flogging. He certainly did, believing that discipline could not

then be upheld without the fear of the lash; and
beyond doubt he was right, for other punishments
had been tried, and the result had been a mutiny;
but he looked forward to the time when such terror
would be unnecessary. Flogging in the Peninsula
was very severe, and Wellington did not shrink
from inflicting it; but, though a stern disciplinarian,
he was not a martinet who stuck rigidly to rule
and made no remissions. All depended upon the
circumstances and the state of the regiment to
which the man belonged. Sir John Moore would
never let off a man under sentence of flogging even
when his officers pleaded for him, saying that,
if men misbehaved themselves, it was the officers
who were to blame, and that he would not
spare the officers the pain of seeing a man punished for their fault. Wellington proceeded on
the same principle, and the result was that, by the
time when he invaded France, he had taught his
officers to do their duty, and that flogging almost
ceased in the army. It is noteworthy that even in
India Wellesley, as he then was, remitted the capital penalty in the case of a murderer who belonged to the Seventy-fourth. So nobly had
that regiment behaved at Assaye that he would
not sully its fair fame by hanging a rogue

who had by chance found his way into its ranks.

Altogether it is idle to contend that Wellington had no care for the private soldier, for considering how small were his powers, he did a great deal for him. Yet he has the discredit not only of neglecting him but of hiding him away in unhealthy countries beyond sea, merely to keep him out of the sight of his countrymen. Lord Wolseley propagated this fallacy, which has really no foundation in fact. It is perfectly true that a shamefully small proportion of the army was at home between 1815 and 1850, and that regiments remained in the Colonies and India for twenty years, and longer, unrelieved. But that was the fault of the House of Commons, which refused to provide an army large enough for the needs of the Empire. The consolidation of India kept the army almost continually on active service from 1814 to 1858; and campaigns—very difficult campaigns some of them—in the Indian climate cost many white men's lives. Then there were wars in Ashanti, in Cape Colony, in China, in New Zealand; and there was always a garrison to be maintained against a possible insurrection of negroes in the West Indies, where, owing to yellow fever, the life of a battalion, on an average, did not exceed two years. It was not Wellington who hid away the army, but the army that was withdrawn from Wellington. This state of things has been remedied in great measure by the establishment of armed native police in the Colonies; and all the police of the Empire are really copied from Wellington's Metropolitan Police.

Finally, it is urged that Wellington is responsible for the British officers' habit of wearing plain clothes when off duty. Undoubtedly Wellington did not like scarlet and gold lace. In the field he never wore anything but a plain blue or grey frock-coat by way of uniform, and would canter round his cantonments in the Peninsula in plain clothes. He even drove out from Brussels to rejoin his army after Waterloo in plain clothes. Moreover, he tolerated a good deal of slovenliness and irregularity in dress on active service, confessing plainly that the sentries at the door of his headquarters, and even the Blues after a few months in the Peninsula, were so much the reverse of smart that they would certainly be sent to drill if they were in England. Quite possibly this was a mistake and bad for discipline; but, in the days when regiments were clothed by their colonels, the troops were often inevitably ragged and dirty though their arms were spotless.

[293]

Still the people who really drove the British officer out of uniform were the two Houses of Parliament and King George IV. Veteran officers could not form a club—the United Service Club—in order to obtain a cheap dinner, but Parliament must accuse them of a military conspiracy. A general officer could not ride down Piccadilly in plain clothes followed by an orderly in uniform, but Parliament must cry out that a debauched soldiery was dragooning freeborn Englishmen. Individual hysterics are trying, but Parliamentary hysterics, recorded in the cold pages of *Hansard's Debates,* are positively insufferable.

However, with the King's uniform thus interpreted as a menace to liberty, officers naturally eschewed it. And they had another reason. George IV was above all things a tailor, and exhausted his sartorial imagination in devising new fancy dress for the army. Officers literally were not sure from one quarter to another of the changes and additions to uniform. The expense was very great. A shower of rain during royal escort-duty might cost an officer of light dragoons from three to four hundred pounds. Moreover the clothes, besides being covered with gold lace, were very tight, very heavy, and not such as a man would

wear for a moment longer than he could help. It
may be said that the Duke should have intervened
to avert such folly; but he wisely refrained from
entering into sartorial controversies with his royal
masters, and from thus wasting the influence which
was needed for more serious matters. Therefore
it was that, when a preposterous shako of royal design was modelled for the infantry, the Duke put
a specimen upon his own head, wore it for several
hours and declared that it would do very well.
George IV's fashions continued, with slight modi-
fications, until the Crimean War, when the British
public was scandalised to hear, through a news-
paper correspondent, that the officers discarded
uniform for plain clothes directly they came off
duty. It was only natural that they should have
done so, since their uniform did not provide ac-
commodation for a handkerchief, much less for
any bulkier article. They would have made no
objection to wearing such reasonable clothing as
the modern khaki. The Duke's example may have
counted for something in the British officers'
preference for plain clothes, but the real reason for
it were comfort and economy.

For the rest, the Duke, though he may not often
have expressed his opinion in public, never failed

to take a keen interest in the army, and was always unhappy over the starving of it by Parliament, knowing better than any other man the appalling danger to which it exposed the country. But all his representations to successive governments on the subject were ignored, and it was not until 1846 that, under Palmerston's inspiration, Ministers at last took up the question seriously. He then wrote a very strong private letter to Sir John Burgoyne, who had served under him as engineer in the Peninsula, upon the whole subject; and this letter having, to the Duke's great annoyance, found its way into the newspapers, greatly strengthened the Government's hands in pushing forward their measures, the chief of which, the re-creation of the militia, was especially recommended by the Duke himself.

Changes in the administration of the army he frowned upon. Twice, in 1837 and in 1849, he opposed, with success, a proposal to transfer the control of the Commissariat from the Treasury to the Ordnance Office, and of the Ordnance Office to the Commander-in-Chief, placing a single Secretary of State, with a seat in the Cabinet, at the head of all. His objection to this plan was that it would transfer the effectual command of the army from the Sovereign to the House of Commons, and that its discipline would in consequence be impaired. He remembered the days before the Duke of York became Commander-in-Chief, when beyond question the discipline of the officers did suffer very seriously from the practical supremacy of the Secretary at War. However, the change has long since been accomplished, with the result that the very title of Commander-in-Chief has been abolished, and that a civilian and a politician is now in undisputed control of the army. How far military discipline may thereby be affected in future, only time can show. It is only certain that political interference with the government of the army is most pernicious, and that in the past fifty years both politicians and the House of Commons have, deservedly or undeservedly, sunk steadily lower in the public esteem.

Other minor military changes Wellington treated with a more open mind. He at first discouraged the introduction of the new priming, which was presently to be developed into the percussion-cap, for an improved musket, having satisfied himself by personal experiments with fowling-pieces that the old-fashioned flint-lock, with its priming of powder, recovered efficiency more quickly after a shower of rain. But the percussion-cap was adopted for the whole army in 1839, and when, some years later, a still greater novelty, the Minié rifle, was introduced, Wellington in person went down to witness the experimental trials of the new weapon, and perceived its merits at once. With his warm approval the Minié rifle was adopted for the British infantry, his only stipulation being that it should be called a musket and not a rifle, lest the whole British army should clamour to be dressed in green.

In the matter of officers he preferred men of gentle birth with some independent means of their own, and steadily discountenanced any increase of the subaltern's pay lest other classes should be tempted to compete for commissions. In these days, when the meaning of the word gentleman is hardly understood except by those in the decline of life, such an attitude seems astonishingly narrow-minded; and yet it is indisputable that youths, born to a certain social position and to the unconscious exercise of command, obtain without effort as officers a readiness of obedience from their men that is beyond the power of their less fortunate brethren. The fact, curiously enough, is attested by a Peninsular officer who was not one of the privileged, and who, while rightly denying to the well-born any necessary superiority in courage or intellect, admitted with some bewilderment their gift of making discipline easy. As to the education of officers, Wellington spoke lightly of the young gentlemen then produced by the Staff College at Wycombe; but when educating his own sons for the army he insisted strongly upon mathematics, and added "perfect knowledge of modern geography and history, of course." Whether the Staff College at Wycombe then taught anything so practical may be questioned. In the matter of purely military training Wellington evidently preferred regimental duty to any theoretical instruction in strategy or tactics.

Viewing the matter broadly, I think the generally accepted opinion that Wellington took little interest in the army at large, in the officers or men, to be wholly mistaken. The most important measures for the amelioration of the soldier's lot —the institution of good-conduct badges and good-conduct pay—though finally carried by the Whig Minister, Lord Howick, were all of them thought out in the first instance by Sir Henry Hardinge, beyond all question with Wellington's thorough approval, and very likely at his instance.[1]

[1] Unfortunately the correspondence of the first Lord Hardinge, which might throw light on this subject, has perished.

The Duke did not always speak kindly himself of the rank and file, but he would allow no one else to utter a word against them; and, on his rides in the country, he never met a man who had served under him without giving him a sovereign. This is not the act of a man who kicks away the ladder by which he has climbed to great heights.

To pass now to his services in civil life, it must be said that, as a departmental administrator in any office he stood in the very first rank, piercing to the heart of every matter with unerring insight, coming swiftly to his decision, and recording that decision with admirable brevity and clearness. Count Molé was very much at fault when he declared that Wellington could not write. It may, indeed, be conceded that he had no great elegance of style, but in the far more difficult art of arrangement—of marshalling his facts and his arguments in telling array till they marched irresistibly to their conclusion—he was a master. Lucid thought is the first step, indeed the only way, to lucid expression, and Wellington seems to have had the whole of the longest memorandum, no matter how difficult or intricate the subject, perfectly clear in his head before he put pen to paper. He wrote very rapidly, though legibly, and made few erasures. It is very rare to find him striking out the first few words of a new paragraph and beginning fresh; the frequent recurrence of which failing is a sure sign of imperfect knowledge or imperfectly ordered thought. By making it his rule to finish the day's task within the day, he was never clogged by arrears of business. In diplomatic work his transparent honesty and abhorrence of crooked dealing earned him the just encomium of Count Molé.

It has many times been written that his participation in political life at home was a mistake; but his position was such that he could hardly have stood aloof. In any difficulty of State his advice and help were always sought, and his feeling was that he, who had been handsomely rewarded for his services by his country, could refuse no appeal that she could make to him. Pure administration was a delight to him; but he hated the paraphernalia of representative institutions, the muddy froth of speeches at public meetings and the hustings, the turmoil of elections, the wasted time and energy of factious controversy, the intrigues and the tricks, the shuffling and the wire-pulling which are the life and breath of the lower sort of politician. Good government was the end at which he aimed; and this seemed to him to be a poor way by which to arrive at it. As to Reform, if you wanted thirty good men in the House of Commons, you were as likely to obtain them from rotten boroughs as through the suffrages of a big manufacturing town. What did it matter how they became members of Parliament so long as they were fit to sit in it? Again, if the country insisted with threats of violence upon the passing of a certain measure, what did it signify by which administration it were passed? If there were a good and strong government in office, it was better that they should carry the measure through, even though they had previously opposed it, and continue to govern well. Really, in his view, such incidents were of trifling importance. The truly essential thing was to have an honest and skilful driver upon the box and a firm hand upon the reins.

In all this there was at bottom much common sense; but such an attitude betrayed, as Disraeli long ago pointed out, great ignorance of England. Moreover, common sense is not acceptable to the many at any time, otherwise the world would be quieter and less discontented than it is; and least of all is it palatable to a people groaning under depression of trade, high taxation, poverty and distress after the exhaustion of a long war. At such times people clamour for a change, any change that may ease the strain upon their powers of endurance. There is no system of government, law, or administration which is not vitiated by serious defects of one kind or another; and there are never wanting teachers, sincere or insincere, to point out that the removal or the alteration of this or that will bring about the millennium. Of course it will not, and cannot; but if the remedy for which people cry out be prescribed to them, as, for instance, the Reform Bill of 1832, they generally pronounce themselves better, at any rate for a time, after taking it. And the mere sympathy shown in yielding to their cry counts, at any rate, for something. The fact is that a little genial humbug helps much towards the government of men. But Wellington was too honest to have anything to do with such things. He was by no means hard-hearted nor unsympathetic, but he had no faith in the nostrums put forward to heal mischiefs which could only be cured by time and patience. The lowering of the franchise in 1832 was in his view —and he was perfectly right—only the first step to democracy; and, since he declined to admit that

all men are equal, democracy was an abomination
to him. He granted that a true democracy, if
such a thing could be, would be the most powerful
of all governments; but he pointed out truly that
the most powerful governments are the most
tyrannical. As to education, he looked upon it
as positively harmful unless founded on a religious
basis, since it would only train up "a lot of clever
devils." The crop of clever devils among us is
certainly abundant, from whatever cause; and the
most unfortunate result of education has been to
teach a vast number of ignorant people to imagine
that they know something.

Altogether, Wellington's gifts were not such as
to make him a successful ruler of England in the
early nineteenth century. If the gold in California
and Ballarat had been discovered in 1820 instead
of in 1849, many things might have fallen out
differently, and he might have come down to us as
a statesman; but such speculations are unprofitable.
Meanwhile, it must be noted that he was by no
means impervious to new ideas. It is a singular
fact that every new invention in the homelier
matters of life, such as a new umbrella or a new
carriage-apron, was eagerly seized upon and tested
by him; and, in more serious affairs, Edward

Gibbon Wakefield's plans of colonisation, though not submitted to him officially, were most carefully weighed and considered by him and pronounced to be worthy of trial. This is the reason why the present capital of New Zealand is named Wellington; and it may be added that, but for an access of sycophancy among certain of Wakefield's colleagues, the capital of South Australia would not have been Adelaide but Wellington.

Passing lastly to his private life, it must be said, first, that he was satisfied that everything he possessed was the very best of its kind in the world —Strathfieldsaye the best country house; Walmer, which was his as warden of the Cinque Ports, the finest castle; Apsley House the finest mansion in London; and so with his carriages, his horses, his dogs, his guns, and everything that was his. Yet with all this, he had a perfect genius for discomfort; the one luxury which he allowed to himself being a bathroom, which was rare in those days. His own bedroom was plain and bare to the extreme; and his sitting-room at Apsley House, which, without being very large, has no fewer than five doors, is a paradise of nothing but draughts. He rose always early, and, wherever he was, got through an astonishing amount of work of all

kinds in the course of the day. He wrote indefatigably with his own hand, answering every letter
that came to him, however unimportant or absurd,
so punctually that it became a practice for strangers to address him on the most ridiculous subjects
in order to obtain his autograph. In the country
he lived the country gentleman's life, looking
most carefully to the improvement of the estate for
the benefit of his successors', who would be less
wealthy than himself, hunting and shooting. It
need hardly be added that, when he had a party, he
personally showed all the guests to their rooms.
Old-fashioned courtesy made it a rigid rule that the
host should not only receive every guest on arrival,
but speed one at parting, no matter how early in
the morning, giving even a girl of fifteen his arm to
lead her to the carriage; and the Duke was not a
man to fall below the highest standard.

He was the most punctual in his attendance at
his parish church, true to his rule never to preach
what he did not practise. A bishop took him to
task for not going to church in London, and he
answered in a humble spirit that his deafness
prevented him from hearing a word, and that, since
his example was not necessary at Strathfieldsaye,
he thought himself justified in staying at home.

But at heart he was a deeply religious man. "The hand of God was upon me," he said, with awe and reverence, when he spoke of his escaping unhurt from the battle of Waterloo; and he believed it. A code of human ethics unsanctified by the command of the Most High was to him inconceivable. If he wrought well and was trusted above other men for righteousness and integrity, it was because he wrought always as in the sight of the Great Taskmaster's eye.

Apart from work, his principal delight within doors was undoubtedly music. No man who has once been a fiddler, and has laboured at the technical difficulties of the greatest of musical instruments, can ever lose his delight in the work of the whole body of the strings; and Wellington was a subscriber, and a very constant visitor, to the concerts of the Antient Music, which at that time offered the best of the art that was to be found in England.[1] Handel was still the master whose works were principally preferred; and, after all, one may do far worse than listen constantly to Handel. For great parties, whether in London or the country, he would engage the greatest

[1] The Duke's ivory ticket for these concerts is in the writer's possession.

artists from the opera in London to sing at his private concerts. But perhaps the most curious relic of his musical taste is a tiny thin volume of chants and hymn-tunes for the church at Strath-fieldsaye, wherein the constant recurrence of the name Mornington points to his share in the selection. Here, in the old Latin sense, is true piety.

As to other arts, it cannot be said that they had great interest for him. He acquired a fine collection of pictures which he captured from King Joseph, who was carrying them off from Spain, and which were presented to him, when he restored them, by King Ferdinand. He made some additions to it, almost entirely of the Dutch School, which was that which he liked best; so that at least he had his preferences in painting. His great position brought upon him the infliction of a certain number of full-length canvases of royal personages, to which he alluded in terms of no great respect. George IV in Highland costume was no more to him than a "fancy-dress" figure, and Alexander of Russia in uniform, "a corporal." To these his favourite Dutch interiors doubtless afforded welcome relief. For the rest, it must be recorded, with marvel to all of us of later generations, that he might have had the beautiful and historic house of Bramshill for his country mansion, and that he preferred Strathfieldsaye. But a man's taste is generally that of his own time; and the earlier decades of the nineteenth century have left us terrible examples of conscientious work wasted upon hideous designs. Not until the nations looked upon each others' horrors at the Exhibition of 1851 did they realise what they were doing, and begin slowly to improve.

In London the Duke went into society, as it is called, was himself very hospitable, and spared no expense over his own entertainments. Whether he derived thence much enjoyment is another question, but probably he did, for he was fond of young people and of pretty faces. He had many affairs with women, not all of them edifying, for on his first return to England many females threw themselves at his head, and the fact was so notorious that even the caricaturists took note of the gallantry of the Master-General of the Ordnance. Yet, as he said with emphasis, no woman ever loved him. His marriage, as has been told, was not a success; his wife being so tactless as to try to make a display of him, which was the thing that his soul abominated. She was lying dead in Apsley House

when the mob broke his windows in 1831, and he
did not marry again. Had he been so fortunate
as to find the ideal wife, who would have understood him, supplemented his intellectual gifts with
peculiar, not necessarily eminent, intellectual quali-
ties of her own, seized his meaning with rapid
intuition, gained his confidence by showing wise
discretion as well as tact, and made her love the
mainspring not only of her own life towards him,
but, almost unawares, of his life towards her, then
he might have been a very different and a far
happier man. As things were he was fortunate
enough to find two women, Mrs. Arbuthnot and
Lady Salisbury, whom he could count upon as true
friends. With the former of them it is said that he
had been too intimate, but in this case passion made
way for something far deeper and better. The
other friendship was wholly without reproach. To
both ladies he was deeply attached; both were
worthy of his attachment, and both died before him.

On the whole, he stands before us as rather a
lonely figure, though not for that reason forbid-
ding. Children adored him; his servants were devoted to him. He loved to do little acts of kindness, as well as great acts of generosity. He was a
good and whole-hearted friend. When Alava, the

Spanish officer who had long been on his staff in the Peninsula, was driven penniless to England, Wellington took him to his bankers and gave them the simple order to honour his drafts for whatever amount. It never occurred to him to do anything else. Towards the end of his life he took Mr. Arbuthnot, after the death of Mrs. Arbuthnot, to live with him at Apsley House, and found in him not only a devoted friend but a tactful counsellor in many minor matters. But otherwise he seems to have had no real friend among men. Towards Castlereagh, who had upheld him through good and evil report, he felt with no common warmth; and, as his reward, he was chosen to break to Castlereagh the fact that he was mad. "It is my duty to tell you that you are not in your right mind," he said, with characteristic courage and simplicity. And poor Castlereagh, burying his face in his hands, answered, "If you say so, I fear that it must be so." It was no common friendship that could stand such a trial as this.

Nevertheless, he stood unconsciously and perhaps involuntarily aloof from other men. It was not through superiority of rank, or honour, or position, or achievement. He was prouder of being an English gentleman than of holding Field-

Marshal's rank in most of the armies of Europe; and such toys as orders and decorations were to him toys and no more. He had been flattered by kings and emperors, and feared by at least one king, George IV, but, though he showed respect for their rank from his unfailing sense of duty, they were no more to him than other men, and less than any true English gentleman. He broke up the diamond star of an order given to him by one potentate, had the stones set afresh in a jewel and gave it to his daughter-in-law. He held such a position as has no other subject in England. Everyone saluted him; everyone called him "Sir," as though he had tacitly been raised to royal rank. He acknowledged the salutes with two fingers, and went his solitary way. Whether men hooted him or cheered him was a matter of indifference; the hooting, perhaps, gave him some cynical amusement. Public demonstrations bored him. He wanted to be alone.

When old age came upon him, rather by a succession of springs and retreats than by steady creeping advance, he refused to allow that he suffered from infirmity. He rejected help in scrambling up steep places, and insisted on climbing painfully into the saddle without assistance. He had stood alone all his life and would do so to the end. With increasing physical weakness, his natural impatience with the stupidity of his fellow-men deepened into petulance and ill-temper, for which, however, he made amends always to his servants and other inferiors who could not reply to him. But while there was work for him to do, he did it, and when past eighty could still do much of it remarkably well. Not for a moment did his sense of duty fail to the very last.

There is something very pathetic about the bent, shrunken figure of the old man, striving until death to be himself, to depend upon himself, to do everything for himself. It was thus that he had taught his officers and trained his armies in India and in the Peninsula, until, as he said of the latter, he could with them go anywhere and do anything. Now there was no army left to him to train, and politicians were no pupils for him. Who cares to summon up a vision of the leader of the House of Lords, sitting spotlessly neat in white stock, blue frock-coat, white waitscoat and trousers, with folded arms and chin on chest, listening for hours to vapid debates and rising in his turn to speak with harsh voice, vehement tones, and somewhat exaggerated vigour of language? Rather do we recall the lithe figure in the grey frock-coat and low cocked hat, sitting on his thoroughbred horse, calm, cool, imperturbable, while forty thousand men wait with confidence for a word from his lips which, they know, will give them the victory over their enemies.

A great soldier he was and a great administrator, and his stature has been raised rather than diminished by the lapse of seventy years. For though his victories may shrink in importance compared with those of greater scale in modern days, and though his work as an administrator may seem trifling beside that now laid upon a Secretary of State, the spirit that made his armies and inspired his labours will withstand the ravages of endless time. It was the spirit of rightness, of truthful dealing, of unwearied industry, of unfailing obedience, the spirit of a man who feared God and loved his country. It is much to be a great general and a great ruler of men; it is more to be also a great gentleman and a great patriot. It is more than all to exalt for ever in a great nation the standard of discipline and of duty. And this was the mightiest work of Wellington.

THE END